Praise for Oola

"Everyone wants to make their life comprehensively better and here is how. *Oola* is happy inspiration!"

—**Mark Victor Hansen**
co-author of the *Chicken Soup for the Soul* book series

"This book couldn't have come at a better time for me. Life takes us on different routes with ups and downs, and hearing the stories in this book really hit home with me. I have been known as "the runner" my whole life, but, as I get older and reality is setting in that peak competitive years might be behind me, it is up to me to figure out my next move. By reading this book, I now have the 7 F's to help me along the way. I do want to continue to 'Get After It' in life and live the OolaLife and I know I can and will! Thank you for both the kick in the pants and the pat on the back—now off to do my workbook!"

—**Carrie Tollefson**
2004 Olympian, host of *CTolleRun.com*

"Wildly creative, packed with insights, this extraordinary book is a gift for anyone who doesn't want to accept 'ordinary' as the only option for life."

—**Jon Acuff**
Wall Street Journal bestselling author of *Quitter*

"In all my years of playing and coaching in the NFL, I have never seen a better playbook for balancing and growing your life. This book was 70 percent entertaining, 30 percent educational, and 100 percent life-changing. If you desire to have a better life, an OolaLife, then you need to read this book."

—**Brant Boyer**
:h

"As a mother, physician, exercis   n
tantly seeking to find balance i   er

reading this book, I feel inspired, grateful, and recommend this book to anyone looking to seek balance in all areas of life. I want the OolaLife!"

—Dr. DelRae Messer
CEO of *DrDelRaeDetox.com*,
Ms. Fitness Minnesota

"From the boardroom of NBC's *The Apprentice*, to the podium of some of the largest Fortune 500 corporate functions, I thought I had firsthand seen and heard it all on the subject of life mastery. *Oola* provides a personal GPS to enlighten, inspire, and give life direction. This is a must read!"

—Troy McClain
CEO of McClain Companies

"Admittedly, I've never gotten all the way through a self-help book. They always feel too pompous and preachy. After finishing *Oola*, I still don't feel like I've read a self-help book. *Oola* reads more like a collection of kick-ass anecdotes and sincere stories that just happen to have meaningful messages. These two guys—the OolaSeeker and the OolaGuru—aren't telling their stories for selfish reasons. They truly want you to live the OolaLife. *Oola* seems more like the script of a classic 'buddy road-trip' movie than a self-help book. Here, though, is maybe all you really need to know: In one single chapter, you'll get the story of the OolaGuru's matching purple shorts/tanktop outfit right next to the OolaSeeker's tale of the time the cops pulled him out of the car while he was wearing nothing but zebra-striped, bikini-cut undies."

—Steve Lange
award-winning columnist, magazine editor, writer

"I've often heard people say, 'play to your strengths.' I have done that in my life, which has made me a successful singer songwriter. But life not all about singing and songwriting. In fact, very little of life is ab singing and songwriting. I want an OolaLife. I don't want to jus good at my job, and epically fail at everything else. This book is a fantastic read, and extremely helpful in creating the kind of life I think we all want to live."

—Tyrone Wells
critically acclaimed singer songwriter

"*Oola* is not just a great book to read, it is a great book to reference. I will keep it near me while on my path to balance and find my purpose. *Oola* is a way of life. Surf the *Oola* wave!"

—Ms. Flor Villarreal
owner, Panama Surf School

"*Oola* is a masterful and unique approach that contains all that you need to achieve balance in each and every area of your life. Packed full of practical and easy-to-apply principles, you will love the message and the very Oola way in which it is presented. You will love this book!"

—Dr. Daniel T. Drubin
author of *Letting Go of Your Bananas*

"As an athlete I am constantly in pursuit of what makes me stronger. I aim to keep God at the core of all I do. It's impressive and reassuring to read a book that not only emphasizes the importance of faith but also provides me with the tools and inspiration to balance and grow in all key areas of my life. *Oola* totally makes me stronger!"

—Annie Hawkins
international professional soccer player

"*Oola* touched my heart. The OolaSeeker and OolaGuru shared straight from their hearts and personal experiences in a lighthearted but practical way—without compromising the strong message. Inspiring!"

—Roelien Muller
director, Asia Center Foundation

"As a two-time Olympian I can attest firsthand to the effectiveness of the principles and values taught in this book. The three steps to the OolaLife can help anyone looking to reach their full potential. *Oola* is a must-read if you are looking to live a better and more balanced life."

—Zach Lund
Two-time Olympian and Olympic coach

"*Oola's* extremely practical approach will help almost anyone turn an average life into an extraordinary life!"

—Dr. Oudi Abouchacra
CEO, *SeizeYourBestLife.com*

"Dave Braun and Troy Amdahl understand the need for balance in life. And they really 'get it' when it comes to the benefits of fitness and running. They accurately describe the joy and empowerment bestowed by running and how the daily run enhances the rest of life."

—Jeff Galloway
Olympian and author of 22 books on running

FIND BALANCE
IN AN UNBALANCED WORLD

*The 7 areas you need to BALANCE and GROW
to LIVE the LIFE OF YOUR DREAMS*

DAVE BRAUN and TROY AMDAHL

Health Communica.
Deerfield Beach, Florida

www.hcibooks.com
www.oolalife.com

Library of Congress Cataloging-in-Publication Data
is available through the Library of Congress

© 2017 David Braun and Troy Amdahl

ISBN-13: 978-07573-1997-6 (Paperback)
ISBN-10: 07573-1997-1 (Paperback)
ISBN-13: 978-07573-1998-3 (ePub)
ISBN-10: 07573-1998-X (ePub)

Publisher: Health Communications, Inc.
       3201 S.W. 15th Street
       Deerfield Beach, FL 33442–8190

For information, please address the authors at *support@oolalife.com*.

Cover design by Svetlana Uscumlic
Cover graphics by Max Amdahl
Cover photo by Ryan Longnecker
Interior design and formatting by Lawna Patterson Oldfield

*This book is the product of
every challenge and hidden blessing in
my life and dedicated to Ashelyn, Tamaryn,
Tiandra, Brynnae, and Zaren.*

*I love you more than dirt,
always and forever.*

—Dave Braun

*Thank you to God.
This book is dedicated to Kris, Max,
Joelle, Bennett, and Alea.
I am blessed.*

—Troy Amdahl

CONTENTS

Section One:
INTRODUCTION TO OOLA

Not where you want to be in life?
Are you feeling lost, stressed, overwhelmed, or
out of balance? Do you lack purpose in your life?
Now is the time to quit pursuing happy
and start pursuing Oola.

Section Two:
THE 7 F'S OF **OOLA**

Everything you MUST balance and grow to live
the life of your dreams . . . The OolaLife.

Section Three:
OOLA BLOCKERS

Learn to overcome the 7 key traits that block
you from the life of your dreams.

Section Four:
OOLAACCELERATORS

Want to get the life of your dreams faster?
Incorporate these 7 OolaAccelerators into
your life and ignite your journey.

Section Five:
THE 3 STEPS TO THE **OOLA**LIFE

Your daily action plan for living
the life of your dreams.

1 BUS. 2 GUYS.
50 STATES.
1 MILLION DREAMS.

On the cover of this book, you'll see our 1970 VW Surf Bus. You might be thinking, *Okay, that's cool, but why a Surf Bus, and what's with the custom paint job?* While it looks like it is covered with splatter paint, take a closer look. Those are actually handwritten stickers representing the individual dreams and aspirations of tens of thousands of people we have met while traveling the country. Our goal is to change the world with a word (Oola) one sticker at a time. People just like you took a moment to step outside the craziness of life and grab a sticker and a Sharpie to reconnect to what they want for their life—and slapped it to the side of our VW. And with this simple gesture, they started taking action toward making their dreams come true.

In this book, you'll learn about this revolutionary process that is taking the country by storm. We're excited to help you begin this journey, and invite you to share your goals and dreams with us. After completing this book, your goals and dreams will become clear, and the action you need to take will be obvious. We have included a sticker in the back just for you. It is blank now, but on it you will be able to write down the one thing, that if you hit it, holds the power to completely transform your life.

Your dream matters. Because we feel that is how we can change the world with this word, Oola. If you commit to positive change and make it happen, you will naturally inspire those around you. A better you, makes a better family, a better community, and ultimately a better world.

We are grateful to be on this adventure with you. You are more capable than you realize. And your dreams are waiting to be claimed. Whatever your dream, we'd be honored to carry it with us on our VW. Now turn the page, and start your journey to your OolaLife.

INTRODUCTION

THE **CALL**

t is hard to believe it was just three years ago I made The Call. The image in my mind is as clear today as it was then.

Earlier that night, I was sound asleep in my uncomfortable bed at a discount motel. I wasn't on vacation—this was my home. I didn't pay by the night—I paid by the month.

The sound was loud and abrupt. I thought someone was breaking into my room. Startled, I jumped up to see what was happening. I looked out the window and saw the police with a battering ram, breaking into the adjoining room.

This was surreal and deeply humbling at the same time. All I can remember thinking is, *How did I get here?* Just a few short years ago, I had it all. I was a married man with five beautiful kids. I had a successful career, a net worth of over $2 million, and a $1.4 million house at the foothills of the mountains.

How did this happen? How did I end up in this crap motel where most residents pay by the hour?

At that moment, I knew I needed to reach out to someone. I reflected on all the relationships in my past for just the right resource.

I was embarrassed, and wasn't looking to be judged, but rather nudged in the right direction. As dark as everything felt around me, I always maintained a sense that "things are going to be okay." In my core, I just knew I needed to get back on the path that I had strayed from some time ago.

I thought back to my internship fifteen years earlier and a guy I knew back then. You probably know a guy like him. In short, I remember one of our mutual friends tossing him a gold horseshoe about the size of a half dollar and telling him to stick it up his ass so he could have a matching set. You know the guy—lucky with zeros on the end.

Everything he touched seemed to turn to gold. He was just lucky, or so I thought. During my internship, as I spent time talking with him and learning from him, I realized it wasn't luck. He worked hard at keeping his life in balance. He made a conscious effort to grow in the important areas in his life. This reflection reconnected me to the path, the pursuit of Oola. I knew who I needed to call.

I walked outside and looked at my neighbor's door, which was dented from the battering ram. I remember thinking that the door looked like I felt. I walked through the rhythm of the lights from the police car reflecting off the buildings around me and made my way to an alley protected from the wind. I remember it was cold outside, but I was not cold. I was humbled, ashamed, and oddly optimistic all at the same time.

All I can remember thinking is, How did I get here?

I had the phone in my hand, hoping to gain the courage to make that call. I knew this was the call I needed to make. I felt it. With vulnerability I called the OolaGuru.

THE **OOLA**GURU

The call was exactly the call I needed to make at exactly the time I needed to make it. I hadn't spoken with the OolaGuru in quite a while. Miles and months had come between us, and this one phone call revealed how our paths had diverged. At one time we were almost of one mind. We had similar dreams, goals, and aspirations. But while my life hit rock bottom, the OolaGuru seemed to have it all.

The OolaGuru is a very private guy. He's far from shy, but his anonymity is based in humility. He listens more than he talks, and let's just say that he has what most of the world wants. He has always been the guy in the group we looked to when we wanted to up our game, in any category of life.

He was completely debt free by the age of forty, he has been married to the same gal (whom he met in kindergarten, by the way) for more than twenty-seven years, he formally retired at forty-two, and now does what he wants, when he wants.

I remember when he couldn't run a mile. Then he set his mind to it and began running marathons, and even completed an Ironman. He spends a ton of time with his kids and works on his faith, dare I say, faithfully.

His personal passion is travel, and he has been to fifty countries and counting. Sounds like fiction, but he is the OolaGuru.

When I called him, he was at his winter home in Arizona. I did most of the talking, and he did most of the listening. I needed to talk, and he was good at listening. After an hour of dumping my problems on him, all I can remember him saying was, "Well, I think you have found the bottom. The good news is it's only up from here!" He went on to say that where I was in this moment was simply where I was . . . not who I was. That I was designed for greatness.

He then told me a story about how they design a car so you can see both in front of you and behind you. They provide a rearview mirror, which is small but adequate. The front windshield is large and unobstructed. It's designed so you can easily see what's ahead. He pointed out how the views ahead and behind are designed to scale. You do need to look behind you, but only briefly, from time to time. The majority of your energy and focus, however, should be on the windshield in front of you.

In that moment, I learned that my life is the same way. I do need to look at my past, but only briefly from time to time, and only to learn from it. The majority of my time should be spent looking forward, planning where I am going.

THE **PURPOSE**

The purpose of this book is clear. We want to lead you to an OolaLife. We want to show you what Oola looks and feels like and how to get there.

We will define Oola and share our stories regarding our different paths to Oola. The heart of the book is the 7 F's of Oola. Here, we will clearly define the seven areas of life that deserve balance and growth.

We will identify the seven roadblocks that can get in the way of the life you want, and introduce the seven accelerators that can get you the OolaLife faster. We will close the book with the three simple steps to the OolaLife.

We will provide two perspectives to educate, entertain, and inspire you on your journey. One perspective will be from the OolaSeeker, who once had Oola, lost Oola, and is now committed to getting his Oola back.

Another perspective is that of the OolaGuru, who is committed to the OolaLife.

By opening up and sharing our true stories, knowledge, and experiences, we hope to inspire you to pursue a life that is balanced and growing. An OolaLife is worth the effort and pursuit. Please, hear us, that regardless of where you are in life and what's in your rearview mirror, you are worthy of better . . . you are worthy of Oola. Congratulations on this noble pursuit.

SECTION ONE

INTRODUCTION TO **OOLA**

*"No matter what you have done, or failed to do,
you deserve the OolaLife."*

—@OolaSeeker

Oola is simply a life that is balanced and growing in the seven key areas of health and well-being. It can be a noun or a verb. It can be a destination or a feeling. It can be as complex as a life growing and balanced in fitness, finance, family, field, faith, friends, and fun (the 7 F's of Oola), or as simple as a sunset, a quiet book on the beach, or a special moment with a child. It is that place we all shoot for in life. The feeling we experience as we celebrate our successes along the way. In short, Oola is cool.

In this section, we will dig a bit more in depth into Oola. To further help you understand Oola, we show, through our own true examples, what a life In Oola looks like, and compare that to one Out of Oola.

We will also explain how two young guys, almost identical in beliefs, passion, goals, and dreams at one point in their lives, met up years later to find they were in much different places. And how this gap helped confirm the need to repeatedly assess where you are in relationship to your goals, prepare a plan, and follow a path.

WHAT IS **OOLA?**

"Life is like riding a bicycle.
To keep your balance, you must keep moving."

—Albert Einstein

Oo ´• la \ *n. adj.* \ 1 a : derived from the French expression *oh-la-la!* b : a state of awesomeness c : a life that is balanced and growing in the key areas of health, finances, career, relationships and well-being c : a destination *(i.e., getting to Oola)* 2 a : describing actions, insights and goals that lead to a balanced life *(ex: That's so Oola.)* 3 a : the ultimate plan for achieving balance in an unbalanced world.

When your life is In Oola, you're in the zone—everything seems to be going your way. It's like swimming with the current. You're covering maximum ground with minimal effort. It's a sweet spot. If you've ever had a sip of it, you want the entire bottle. It's good—like finding twenty dollars in the couch, getting all green lights, receiving a Christmas bonus in July, having all tweets re-tweeted, easily slipping into your skinny jeans—good!

Oola is experienced when your life is balanced and growing. That is why we have dedicated ourselves to the pursuit of Oola and are committed to sharing it with the world.

The opposite of a life In Oola is a life Out of Oola. Unfortunately, this represents the majority of society. It can be sneaky. On the surface, those with an Out of Oola life may appear to be okay, may even appear to be "winning." It's the guy in the gym with 6 percent body fat who needs a ride home because he can't afford a car. It is the millionaire whose only connection with his kids is their occasional text requesting more money.

OOLASEEKER

My Pink Bike

Growing up on a small farm in North Dakota presents many opportunities to become "a man!"

> **Regardless of where you are in life, there is hope.**

Growing up on a small farm in North Dakota with four sisters (and being on the receiving end of the hand-me-down chain) wasn't one of those opportunities.

And as far as hand-me-downs go, how about your older sisters' three-time hand-me-down pink Huffy three-speed bike? Unfortunately, the color wasn't the only problem. Multiple spokes were missing, the rims were bent and rusty, and the tires were bald and barely holding air.

I am not sure what compelled me to take this bike out on gravel roads, through the pastures, and along the cow trails. What I do know is that the ride wasn't pleasant. On short trips it wasn't a big deal. I always made it to where I wanted to go, with only minor difficulty and pain. However, as the bike evolved into my primary means of transportation on the farm, the ride became depressingly difficult. There were times I was barely moving. I felt stuck in low gear.

My body felt fatigued and tired from all the work. It was painfully rough riding. Many times I felt like just getting off, abandoning the bike, and walking home. And, when I did get home, this misery wasn't just mine; I wanted everyone to share in it. If I wasn't happy, there was no reason for my sisters, parents, or even the dog to be happy.

This pink bike represents a life NOT in Oola. This bike wasn't growing; it was dying. It was not balanced; it was broken. It was the wrong size; it was damaged and out of tune. It was fine for a few pushes of the pedal, but with repetition it was wearing, fatiguing, and frustrating.

This was my life three years ago. Depressed, stressed, tired, and going nowhere. At times, I felt like just abandoning my life and starting over—or worse. My life was out of Oola.

OOLAGURU

Spinning Plates

I have pursued growth and balance in my life for as long as I can remember. I haven't done this because someone told me to, or because I read a book on the topic. I pursued Oola because I saw that it works. Whenever great things were happening to me, my life was balanced and growing. I also noticed that whenever I felt most fulfilled, my life was balanced and growing.

I am kind of a quiet guy, but if someone asks, I'm happy to share my opinion regarding the key to life success. On many occasions, people with a lot more experience and letters after their names will challenge whether it is possible to balance your life. I point out that their analysis is a bit too literal. I am not advocating devoting exactly 205.7 minutes each day to each F of Oola. Much like a marriage is not truly 50–50, it is more like 80–20 . . . sometimes the wife carries 80 percent of the load and other times the husband does the heavy lifting.

My best way of explaining how to reach balance is a story about the guy in the circus who spins the plates. Picture a circus performer entering the center ring with thin poles, each six feet high. For this story, let's say there are seven poles. The performer then grabs shiny white plates. He spins one, much like a basketball player spins a ball on his finger, and balances the spinning plate on the pole. He then does the exact same with the six remaining poles and plates. Usually, by the time he's moved on to pole four or five, his first plate begins to wobble. He then has a choice: "Should I move on to the next plate, or go back to the first plate and spin it again before it wobbles and hits the floor?" For the remainder of the act, we are intrigued by his efforts. He is running back and forth, from wobbling plate to wobbling plate, to make sure none of them fall and hit the floor.

This is exactly how I pursue life balance each and every day. It is impossible to perfectly balance your life in each key area of life. I just wake up each day and make sure my plates are still spinning. And if I notice one is about to hit the floor, I give it a spin.

Regardless of where you are in life, there is hope. The truth is that Oola is a gift available to anyone and everyone. You are reading these words for a reason—you are worthy of a life in Oola. No matter what you have done, or what you have failed to do, Oola is available to you. Go get it!

CHAPTER
2

TWO ROADS
TO **OOLA**

"Sometimes it's the journey that teaches you
a lot about your destination."

— Drake

This is our story. A story of how two guys with similar interests, values, beliefs, and aspirations take two different roads and reunite and share their journey to Oola and share their passion to help others "up their Oola." Here is our personal insight on our journey to this point and beyond.

OOLASEEKER

Everybody Loves a Comeback

There are times that it would have been cooler to be the Guru and not the Seeker.

But under no circumstances would I trade places. I'll gladly hang with his family at his summer lake cabin, use his beach house, and drive his Ferrari, but I am blessed for the life that I have lived thus far. I am blessed for all my experiences—my losses and my wins.

The journey back—especially if you once had a life of Oola— can be difficult and full of challenges. To write about my shortcomings and failures is still tough and not very flattering. I have learned to accept all of it. Let me rephrase, I have come to own, and actually feel blessed, because of it . . . all of it!

You see, the bad news is this story is true. The good news is this story is true.

It is not a tragedy, it is a reality—my reality, which has led me to this point, to the point where I am getting my Oola back and having the opportunity to educate and facilitate Oola to the world. I really hope to change lives by sharing my story. I am not going to lie; I often wonder: What happened along the way to make my journey difficult? What led me to the bottom?

When I evaluate this, it's fairly clear that my life started moving out of Oola when I started feeling cocky about my successes. I needed to be humbled. I lost gratitude for everything. I believed everything I had was because of me and no one else. With the loss of humility and gratitude, I made several choices that eventually led to feelings of guilt and self-sabotage. These OolaBlockers knocked me off my perch, threw me out of balance, and the plates started dropping one by one. My marriage started to fail and soon I was divorced, broke, living in a motel, and driving my mom's crappy old Taurus. Yes, I said it—my mom's car.

Everybody loves a comeback—especially if you're the one coming back.

Everybody loves a comeback—especially if you're the one coming back. In this story, that's me. That phone call three years ago to the OolaGuru started my journey back to Oola. What a ride it's been. I removed the OolaBlockers and started to incorporate all the OolaAccelerators. My life changed quickly, but only with focused action and serious effort. I know that if I can do it, so can you.

Whatever has compelled you to pick up this book and get you to Chapter Two will be the same inspiration that will help you finish this book, remove the OolaBlockers, and add the OolaAccelerators to start your journey to balancing and growing your life . . . a life of Oola!

OOLAGURU

The Photo Album

Have you ever been to a friend's house and looked at their photos? Photos serve as snapshots of our lives, special occasions, milestones, vacations, parties . . . the highlights.

In all fairness, this book is a bit of a photo album. It will point out all of the highlights of my life in the seven key areas of life (the 7 F's of Oola). I am not a real guru. Not even close. I do not possess unique gifts or talents. I am a T-shirt and comfy jeans guy—no different than you; nothing special.

One of my favorite sayings of all time is, "I am not yet the man I want to be, but thank God I am not the man I used to be." I have not been without my challenges.

Life delivers challenges to all of us, even the "gurus." For me, challenges represent a chance to learn and reveal our true character. It is easy to have a smile on your face if you are sitting on the beach at your vacation home. Your true character is revealed when you're faced with adversity. Sometimes I was happy with myself and how I handled my own personal challenges. Other times, not so much.

On the contrary, the OolaSeeker is not a failure. In fact, he is one of the most positive, kindhearted, creative, and talented people I have ever met. Our goals and dreams in life have always been almost identical. That is why when we reconnected three years ago, we were curious to discover why we were at such different points in life. Digging into this revealed the differences between us. Over time I made more of the choices, and developed the traits, that propelled my life forward and put me on the fast track. We call these OolaAccelerators.

We also noticed that the OolaSeeker had drifted into a ratio of more traits that blocked his life progression. We call these OolaBlockers. This insight was huge in furthering my personal growth and in helping the OolaSeeker get back on the right path.

As you progress through this book, you will at times relate to the OolaSeeker and at times connect with the OolaGuru. James Truslow Adams once said, "There is so much good in the worst of us, and so much bad in the best of us, that it ill behooves any of us to find fault with the rest of us."

We all experience our wins and our losses, successes and failures. This book does not judge. Our goal is to provide different perspectives to relate to, learn from, and grow. Discover where you are, connect with your desire to be better, eliminate your OolaBlockers, and pump up your OolaAccelerators and pursue the life you desire. It is our hope that by sharing our successes, failures, knowledge, and experiences, we can help you get to Oola faster.

THE SEVEN F'S
OF **OOLA**

"Everything in life . . . has to have balance."

— Donna Karan

Welcome to the heart of the book. An understanding of the 7 F's of Oola is mandatory if you desire to have the life of your dreams.

Each F represents a key area in life. They are: fitness, finance, family, field, faith, friends, and fun. Volumes of books have been written on the importance of each category and how to improve in each F in explicit detail. This is not our goal. Our goal is to educate and entertain you and provide enough information that you realize these areas of life are worthy of your attention.

We will also define each F, offer some insight from our life experience on how to grow in each F, and provide some solid principles and tips to help you up your Oola in the categories that feel low.

As you read through these categories, begin the process of self-assessment. Ask yourself: In which F's am I strong? In which am I weak? Am I balanced? By starting to answer these questions now, you will be better prepared for the final section where we outline the 3 Steps to the OolaLife.

Here is the 33,000-foot flyby:

1) **OOLA**FITNESS is everything health and wellness in your life. However, we are primarily referring to how you use your body and what you put into it.

2) **OOLA**FINANCE is personal finance and includes income, spending, debt (very UnOola), charitable giving, and saving/investing.

3) **OOLA**FAMILY is all things family. Single, committed, married, divorced, kids, stepkids, extended family . . . all belong here.

4) **OOLA**FIELD is your career, your profession. Stay-at-home parents, this includes you. We feel being a stay-at-home parent is very Oola. Students are also in this category.

5) **OOLA**FAITH is based on gratitude and humility and an understanding of our greater purpose in the world. Your faith is personal, but you can't have an OolaLife without having a higher purpose for your life and making this F of Oola a priority.

6) **OOLA**FRIENDS is everything social. And, yes, even the toxic relationships need to be addressed in this F of Oola.

7) **OOLA**FUN explores your personal passion in life. This includes having a little fun every day and making sure you have a plan to check items off your "bucket list" long before the inevitable happens.

OOLAFITNESS

Eat less than you burn or burn more than you eat . . . your choice!

*"Take care of your body.
It's the only place you have to live."*

— *Jim Rohn*

T
he word "fitness" has taken on a new direction over the last twenty years. It has been so overused that its meaning has been diluted to the point of near irrelevance. The term fitness has lost all its beauty and appeal.

Today, the term seems to be used in two ways. The first definition centers around how your health affects everything you do. This is about feeling good, looking good, being healthy, and being productive. It's about how you move your body and what you put in your body. This is the skinny jeans fit, I feel sexy, I am going to take on the world kind of fitness . . . this is OolaFitness!

The second definition is the crap you see and hear in the media and on the web. Take this pill, drink this juice, be skinny by your reunion, size two by tomorrow, and shake this weight to a leaner, fitter you—really! Very non-Oola.

Here is a good question: Is growing your fitness difficult or easy to do?

Here's a good answer: It's simple, but it's not easy. If you consume more than you burn, your body will store it. If you burn more than you consume, your body will shed it. You also need to pay attention to the quality of what you consume.

Sounds simple, but trust us, it is not easy. Look around you. If you live in a city you are never more than one block from a quick 2,000-plus empty calorie meal. If you live in a small town or in the country, and have a microwave and a freezer, those same 2,000-plus empty calories are available to you in three minutes.

Even if you try eating healthy, getting proper nutrition, and exercising on a regular basis, you can end up throwing all your efforts out the window with a couple stops at the coffee shop for that amazing frozen coffee or hitting up the tasty salty fries, a burger, and a Coke

If you are reading this chapter and are looking for the next quick fix, the next ThighMaster, or screaming, ponytailed trainer running like a gazelle, you are not going to find it.

on the way home from work.

We get this. We love good food, we love our coffee, and we love hanging with the kids and enjoying a good movie, New York style pizza, and M&Ms in our popcorn. So, yes, simple—but not easy!

If you are reading this chapter and are looking for the next quick fix, the next ThighMaster, or screaming, ponytailed trainer running like a gazelle, you are not going to find it. But, if you are looking for simple concepts, powerful knowledge, and inspiration that can help you grow your OolaFitness . . . then keep reading—you are on the right track.

OOLASEEKER

Chick Tendencies

I am the first to admit that I have "chick" tendencies. Maybe it was growing up with four sisters or raising my four daughters, but somewhere along the way I became self-conscious of my body.

Now if you are a woman, don't go crazy on me for using the phrase chick tendencies—I mean that with the greatest amount of respect. But, you have to admit that you are the one who buys Spanx to hold in this or bras that push up that. You spend an hour in front of the mirror and put on shoes that make you four inches taller.

If you are a dude, please back off with your snickering—you have your own little secrets and issues, go deal with those and just respect that I get to be—or should I say have to be—a little transparent to get my point across.

Let me explain, I work hard at fitness because of two simple reasons. First, my chick tendencies: I can't stand when my belly even thinks about hanging over the front of my pants. Just the slight feeling of skin inching its way forward pisses me off and makes me feel fat. (Man, I am a chick.) Screw it, let's keep going. Maybe this will be therapeutic. At times, I can literally feel that my boobs might be jiggling a touch when the car ride is bumpy. And that is when I want to immediately stop and rip out a hundred push-ups. I will never have a double chin—ever!

Second, I have so much to accomplish in life and there is no way that I am going to let not being fit, having low energy, or feeling old get in the way of accomplishing my goals and doing what I love. I will not let being lazy in fitness keep me from playing soccer with the kids, running around with the grandkids someday, or trekking the world.

Every ounce of sweat and every time I pass the coffee shop without stopping is worth it because of those two reasons. One reason is superficial in nature and one more deep and meaningful, but both of these triggers keep me growing my OolaFitness.

So, is fitness really that important in accomplishing all of this? Maybe you are overweight and thinking, "I am happy with the way I look. I can play basketball with the kids and I am totally cool with my productivity." That's all good.

But let me tell you about a little experiment to offer some clarity. Since I am the risk-taker who sometimes tries strange things, I wanted to see what would happen to a fit, thirty-nine-year-old guy who just lets it all go. What would happen to my fitness and my pursuit of my OolaLife if I just quit working out for forty days and ate whatever I was craving? Let the experiment begin: In forty days I gained twenty-six pounds and started having heartburn, increased blood pressure, and dangerous cholesterol levels. My sex drive went from Ferrari to Vespa and all of the plates started to wobble . . . all of them! It was my test to see if it mattered. It matters in a big way! Keep this F in check, be real to who you are and where you are. Find your personal triggers that help you grow your fitness to new levels.

OOLAGURU

My First Run to the Mailbox

In 2004, I couldn't run a mile. In fact, I couldn't run to the mailbox. It was my inability to run to the mailbox that started me on my path to grow my OolaFitness. I was at the lake. The mailbox is not attached to the cabin; it is down the winding gravel road maybe a half a mile away. Focused on college and then career, my level of fitness had faded incrementally each year. The slide happened slowly, or at least not quickly enough for me—or those around me, I hoped—to notice. But my fitness level was deteriorating nonetheless.

It was kind of like when you see an old friend for the first time in ten years. You look at them and think, "Wow, they've sure aged and gained weight." For some reason, you don't realize your long-lost friend is probably thinking the exact same thing about you.

I woke one morning and had letters to mail. I would usually hop on my ATV and take the letters to the mailbox. The voice in my head had been talking more as of late. It was more like two voices, kind of like that classic scene with John Belushi in *Animal House*. The good voice was telling me how fit I was. "You're not bad for your age. You're not nearly as big as him or him. You're the man. Remember back in high school when you could . . ."

The bad voice was telling another story. "Dude, you're getting fat. It is happening to you. You have a belly and are developing boobs. I'm afraid you're going to start lactating."

It was time to settle the conflict. I left the ATV in park and put on my running shoes (actually, more like whatever shoes I had in the closet). I strapped them on and headed to the mailbox . . . running. On the slight uphill, maybe halfway there, I was done. I stopped, bent over, grabbed my knees, and rounded my back to get more air into my lungs. I was toast and very humiliated. That was the moment I was confronted with the reality of my deteriorating health.

Since the "run" sucked, I figured I needed to truly assess my fitness. I decided to blow the dust off the scale and see what it said. So I hopped on the scale and it read "198," which was probably 35 pounds over my ideal weight. Also, it was dangerously close to 200. Too close for my comfort.

When people get to this point in their lives, they seem to do one of two things. Some throw their hands in the air and ascribe to the philosophy of "You only live life once. I'm going to live it the way I want to." And by "live it the way I want to," they really mean "I'm going to slowly deteriorate, gaining a few pounds each year, until one day I look up and I'm taking injections for diabetes, pills for hypertension, and shopping at specialty stores for clothes."

It happens to the best of us. Thankfully, I was not in that group. I chose the other path. I was going to make a change. The "198 moment," combined with my inability to run to the mailbox, fueled my motivation to commit to improving this area of my life. And when I commit, I commit. My family claims I do not have a dimmer switch. I'm either "on" or "off." My fitness switch was now "on."

It was early summer and I committed to running the Chicago Marathon in the fall. I researched how to train for and complete a marathon without injury. I created and stayed disciplined to a plan based on what others had used to succeed. I ran 613 miles in 18 weeks. I ran whenever I could find the time. Before the sun came up. After the sun went down. I ran in 40-degree rain and 100-degree heat. I suffered through every kind of injury. I strained muscles I didn't even know I had. I lost six toenails.

And this is definitely one of my "If I can do it, anyone can" examples. I am definitely not a natural athlete. My only competitive sport in high school was golf, and I only participated in that because I could play for free. I barely made the team.

But when it came to running a marathon, I'd made a promise to myself, and I committed to keep it.

It worked. On October 10, 2004, I completed my first marathon in a time of 3:54. Respectable. When I arrived home, my youngest daughter innocently asked, "Daddy, did you win?" After a pause, and contemplating whether finishing 8,758th felt like a victory, I simply said, "Yes."

A few weeks later, as the pain of the training faded, I realized what a great experience it had been. I felt great, I lost nineteen pounds, and redefined what I believed to be a challenge and, more important, what was possible.

To this day I continue to grow my OolaFitness. Since 2004, I've run sixteen marathons. I quit counting. I merged my tolerance of running with my love of travel by running marathons in other countries. In Greece, I ran the original marathon from Marathon to Athens. In Nairobi, I ran with Kenyans. With the challenge of a marathon fading with repetition, I set my sights on a full-distance Ironman. For exercise newbies, that's a 2.4-mile swim, followed by a 112-mile bike, and then a 26.2-mile run. I earned the title of "Ironman" in 2010. I used the term "earned" because, trust me, if you complete an Ironman, you've earned it. That was a one-time event for me. I have great respect for the discipline required to complete such a task.

This from a guy who, just six years earlier, couldn't run from the cabin to the mailbox.

◎   ◎   ◎   ◎

The benefits of fitness are numerous and transcend the category. Fitness is huge. If you make a commitment to continue to grow in this category, not only will you have the obvious health benefits, but you will also have more energy, your mood will improve, you will look better, you will sleep better . . . The benefits are countless and worth your pursuit.

OOLAFITNESS TIPS

1) Keep It Simple

Do not get caught up in the hype and quick fixes. Anything worth doing is worth doing right. Growing your OolaFitness is worth all of the blood, sweat, and tears. If you are committed, you will likely experience all three—literally!

2) Work Harder

When you decide to work out, go for a bike ride, or play soccer in the backyard with the kids, bring it! There are opportunities to get accidental exercise every day. Fitness does not only occur in a gym. Remember: Burn more than you eat. The harder you work and the harder you play, the more you burn!

3) Eat Smarter

Soda, fries, sugar, and excessive breads/whites = bad. Fruits, vegetables, lean meats, nuts, and legumes = good. Don't pretend that you don't know how to eat healthy and don't self-sabotage this. Eat because you are hungry and for fuel only. Don't eat to feel better or because you are bored. Make healthier food choices and eat less than you burn.

Think of fitness as a journey and not a destination. Envision a lifetime of looking good and feeling good sprinkled with occasional family pizza nights, enchiladas and margaritas with friends, and lazy days on the couch. The key word is "occasional." The rest of the time you need to simplify. Eat less than you burn and burn more than you eat!

OOLAFINANCE

Spend Less Than You Make

"Winning with money is more about doing the small things consistently, than doing the big things intermittently."

— @OolaGuru

OolaFinance and OolaFitness have a lot of similarities. In OolaFitness, we advocate "burn more than you consume." In OolaFinance, we simply want you to "spend less than you make." Both very simple conceptually. Both very difficult to execute.

Debt is always the pink elephant in the room when discussing personal finance. Debt sucks. Debt is not Oola. We hate debt. We eliminate what we hate, therefore we worked to dig out of debt. It wasn't easy or quick. But it was worth it.

The problem with debt is that it is so socially prevalent it is deemed normal. Debt is not normal. Historically, in fact, debt is a relatively new phenomenon. Just look back a generation or two. Our grandparents paid for everything in cash. The only exception was getting a loan to buy a home. Fast forward a generation. Our parents would justify getting a loan for a home, cars, and maybe the occasional vacation or home improvement project. Now fast forward to today. I saw a guy charge a cup of coffee at the gas station. That is ridiculous.

Be responsible with the money entrusted to you. Dr. Danny Drubin speaks about the "dash in life" in his book *Letting Go of Your Bananas*. He reflects upon a walk through a cemetery and noticing all the words and numbers etched in granite at the foot of each grave. He looked closer and noticed the dash between the numbers.

This lead to the realization that the dash in life is fleeting, and what you do during that dash is what really matters. Dr. Drubin writes, ". . . make the most of each day by letting go of everything that does not figure into the brighter future you envision for yourself." Use your time on this planet wisely—seize the dash.

The same can be said for money. You enter with none, you leave with none. Money will come and money will go during the dash. You

Our budget back then had a category called "fun money." It was $15 for the entire month.

will make some, you will spend some, and hopefully you will give some (giving is very Oola!). It is what happens during the dash that matters most. If you do good things with money, you will attract more. If you are reckless and irresponsible with money, you will quickly find yourself with none. Be a good steward of the money entrusted to you.

The whole point of Oola is to balance and grow. To grow your OolaFinance you must learn. We know a guy who has a six-year degree in archaeological artifacts from the sixth century A.D. He is really smart on that topic. The problem is he can't balance his checkbook or even grasp the concept of a budget. It is possible to get through life just fine without knowing the significance of an etching on a broken plate from 587 A.D. You cannot slip through life and be stupid on the subject of money or the OolaLife will pass you by. The more you know, the more you learn, the more responsible you will be, and the more that will flow your way.

OOLASEEKER

A Date with Halle Berry

Ask a man the popular question: "If you could have a date with any woman in the world, who would it be?" You will get a wide range of answers from Queen Elizabeth to Fiona from Shrek (yes, I heard that once). But, hands down, the most common answer is Halle Berry . . . Halle Berry! Their answer is usually followed up with what they would talk about, what they would do on the date, and how much Halle Berry would fall in love with them.

But honestly, the majority of these men wouldn't have a clue what to do if Halle Berry walked into a restaurant, sat down next to them, and said, "Hi, I am Halle." The first thing they would most likely do is call their best buddy to let him know what's going down. Next, they would take a picture to prove to their buddy that it was really Halle Berry. After immediately posting the photo to Facebook, they would likely fail to utter a single word of conversation, mentally save any memories, and might even start to feel uncomfortable that she is there. Before you know it, she would leave and they would never have a chance to go on a date with her again.

When I started making large amounts of money in my late twenties, each paycheck was like a date with Halle Berry—not a clue what to do with it. I didn't know how to manage it or save it, and, just like Halle Berry, it would soon leave my life.

I never learned about money growing up. "It is the root of all evil" and "it cannot buy happiness" were the consistent themes of my earliest money memories.

After hitting bottom and losing Oola three years ago, I have put much focus on learning everything I can about finance. I was confident I would get my Oola back; I was confident I would get the money back. Of all the stressors I faced at the bottom of the barrel, the lack of money and the large amounts of debt were killers. After working extremely hard and smart, I am proud to say that I am well on my way to becoming debt free and securing my future for myself and my family.

Simply put, if you take care of money, it will take care of you.

OOLAGURU

The Joneses Don't Know Jack

Success, like it or not, is often defined in society by the material: what we drive, where we live, what we do. If it is your goal to pursue a life in Oola, you must first challenge many of the commonly accepted definitions of one dimensional/material success that are continually embedded into our subconscious by our culture and media.

We are a society seemingly obsessed with stuff and racing to keep up with the Joneses. He Who Dies with the Most Toys Wins . . . are you kidding me? Don't get me wrong, I like some nice stuff, I have some nice stuff, but the key word is "some." Keep it in check; keep it in balance and in proportion to where you are financially. There will always be bigger, better, faster, and stronger. We need to temper our pursuit of only stuff, since the pursuit of stuff is often a self-indulgent and empty journey. Please don't hear me saying that you need to shave your head, join a monastery, and swear off all things material. Keep some of your toys, but kindly keep it in perspective and in proportion; it is just stuff, after all. All I ever noticed as I began to accumulate more and more stuff was that it only made for more to maintain and sort through for our semiannual trip to Goodwill.

Personally, I've always run my own race since as long as I can remember. I was unconcerned with the Joneses. In my junior year in college I wrote out my goals. "DEBT FREE BY AGE 40" was at the top of the list.

I may have been born with a "horseshoe up my ass," but I was not born with a silver spoon in my mouth. We were not poor; we were well provided for but far from rich.

It was made clear to us kids at a young age that we would have all of our financial needs met until we completed high school, but, after that, we were on our own. Some believe that your first memory relating to money has a great impact on your financial path. That was my first memory, and that simple message stuck. I am grateful for that lesson. My two sisters and my brother and I all found a way to go out in the world and provide for ourselves and our families with no assistance.

I got married during my last year of college. We were young and made our share of money mistakes. I graduated college with more than $55,000 in student loans, and that was a while back. My wife had loans as well. We took out loans on cars we shouldn't have bought. I purchased our first home with no money down. In fact, I got a check at closing because my uncle was a Realtor who gave me his commission back. Much of my so-called Guru Wisdom was not learned in a book, but on the street, like in these examples of bad choices.

Thankfully, the economy was good then and we didn't get our financial heads taken off. As we learned from our mistakes and from the knowledge of others, we started to implement changes, slowly made progress, and pointed our financial life in the right direction.

Dave Ramsey, a bestselling author and radio show host on the topic of personal finance, refers to this as "a Crock-Pot versus a microwave" method. We were definitely on the Crock-Pot financial plan in those early years, and our Crock-Pot was stuck on low. Many times it seemed as if we were making no progress, but we continued to pound down debt any way we could. We just felt we were on the right path. Since all of our extra money was spent to pound down debt, those were not luxurious times. To paint a bit of a picture, our cars during this period were two Pintos (one blew up) and a $500 yellow Ford Fairmont. The Fairmont was so ugly we named it

Bingo because it looked just like a car a cute little old blue-haired grandma might drive to the bingo parlor.

I saved the change in the ashtray each year to take my wife out for her birthday at our favorite pizza joint (our kids still don't believe this story). Our budget back then had a category called "fun money." It was $15 for the entire month. Eating out was considered fun, so it didn't go far. The funny thing is, as I reflect on this chapter of my life, I do so with fondness and a smile on my face. Those were special times.

Overcoming challenges builds character and creates respect. Much in the same way, years later, we have the greatest respect for our coaches and teachers who challenged us the most. I attribute the process of my wife and I working together toward a common goal in the early stages of our marriage as one of the keys for the success we now feel so grateful to experience.

We kept the Crock-Pot cooking, pounding down the debt, day by day, month by month, year by year. Then we looked up one day and we were there. On the eleventh month of my fortieth year, I wrote my last check to the bank. We were debt free, houses and all! It was surreal. It was gone. The best way I can describe it is we felt lighter.

Nothing I have ever purchased has felt as good as being debt free feels. It took fifteen years. My wife and I made a vow to never borrow money again, for any reason. We don't even have credit cards. We're that passionate about the topic.

We share our story not to boast, but to show you what's possible. It's not easy, but it is possible. The only advice I can give based upon our fifteen-year journey to becoming debt free is quit racing the Joneses; they don't know Jack! Instead, begin a race against yourself. Use your previously misdirected energy and misdirected money to do better than your former self. I once heard, "There is no nobility in proving one's superiority to another (i.e., the Joneses); true nobility comes from improving upon your former self." If insurmountable debt is your issue, give it a beatdown and tackle it the same way you would eat an elephant: "One bite at a time!"

I know firsthand the sacrifices you will need to make to eat this elephant. You will have to deny yourself and your family the things the Joneses buy. Just know that if you listen to anyone with common wisdom, you will quickly learn that true life success cannot be achieved by material trophies. True life success comes from fulfillment. Fulfillment is best explained by a quote from Lao Tzu's *Tao Te Ching*:

> *If you look to others for fulfillment, you will never truly be fulfilled. If your happiness depends on money, you will never be happy with yourself. Be content with what you have; rejoice in the way things are. When you realize there is nothing lacking, the whole world belongs to you.*
> *P.S.: Don't go into debt . . . (I added this last part).*

OOLAFINANCE TIPS:

1) **No Debt**

Debt is a burden. Debt is evil. We'll let a mortgage on a primary home slide, but that is it, and only if the numbers are right. Trust us on this one, we have both had debt and have not had debt. Life is much better without debt. This is a tough one, but chip away—the financial security reaped at the end of the process is sweet.

2) **Be a Good Steward of the Money**

Take care of the money that comes your way. This is being a good steward, or manager, of the money you are blessed with. We came to this planet with no money and we will exit the same way. If you do good things and are responsible with the money that comes your way, more will come your way. We have experienced this firsthand.

3) **Learn**

Don't put your head in the sand. Pay attention; learn about money. The resources are plentiful. Track what's coming in and what's going out. Make a budget. Plan ahead. Save for emergencies and high-dollar projects around the corner (vacations, holidays, college, wedding, etc.). One good starting point is Dave Ramsey's book, *The Total Money Makeover*.

OOLAFAMILY

Love. Lead. Commit.

"My family is my strength and my weakness."

—Aishwarya Rai Bachchan

F amily is defined as anyone related by blood, marriage, or adoption. These are the people you interact with regularly. In some cases, whether you like it or not.

If you identify a toxic relationship with a friend and you decide to call it quits, you simply don't respond to their email, block their number, unfriend them on Facebook, and move on with your life. With family, it's a bit more complicated.

Parents, children, extended family, co-this, and step-that . . . all are permanently in the family category. Where should you focus your energy on growth in this category? There are so many relationships and different dynamics with each one.

We advocate looking at your family relationships like a series of rings, with the center ring representing the core. Picture a series of additional rings that get slightly larger as they expand outward. The core relationships are those that are dearest to you. If you're married, this would likely be your spouse and kids. If you are single, it may be siblings or parents.

You may be able to sprinkle in that special grandparent, aunt, or cousin in this core ring as well. You define who is in your core.

As the rings expand out, the relationships are still family but progressively less connected. Aunts, uncles, and cousins would be examples of second-ring family relationships.

The third ring and beyond can represent distant relationships. People you are related to, but contact may only consist of the occasional wedding announcement, holiday card, or invitation to a reunion.

As you walk though this exercise, you can probably feel the intensity of the emotions ease from the core to the distant rings. Family relationships are powerful. As with any form of power, it can be used for good or for evil.

Family relationships are powerful. As with any form of power, that power can be used for good or for evil.

If you can harness the pure love from healthy family relationships, you will grow in this category and progress toward Oola.

However, we have to offer a word of caution. Toxic relationships love to hang out in this category. In working toward Oola, you must identify these toxic relationships and deal with them. Whether it is establishing proper boundaries or offering forgiveness related to previous pain, confront the issue. Otherwise, relational toxicity will sneak into your core ring, spread like a virus, demand attention, and suck the focus from your healthy core family relationships.

OOLASEEKER

There IS Life After Divorce

Jeff Foxworthy is estimated to have a net worth of 100 million dollars and is best known for his "you might be a redneck if" jokes. This past Christmas, I was resting in the living room and I could overhear my nephews, nieces, and some of my kids making up their own redneck jokes. Out of sheer post-Christmas dinner fatigue, laziness, and boredom, I started twisting their jokes and thinking of my own. I had some really good ones. For instance, if your car is being towed away and there is nothing mechanically wrong nor was it parked illegally . . . you may be low in OolaFinance. If you have ever financed a tattoo with no money down and zero interest for twelve months . . . you may be low in OolaFinance. If none of your shirts covers your stomach and they are designed to . . . you may be low in OolaFitness.

The list goes on and on, but my favorite, mostly because it hit close to home was, "If the words co-parent or former spouse are new titles that describe you . . . you may be low in OolaFamily!" The funny part of this is that I really had no idea that those terms existed until my divorce classes. Yeah, you have to take divorce classes! I'd obviously heard the term "ex-wife," but never the former spouse/coparent thing. I thought it was quite funny that they now have politically correct terms for people going through a divorce. The reality of the situation was that I had much to learn about going through a divorce—pre and post.

I didn't grow up around divorce and the mere thought of it was instantly associated with weakness and failure. I was raised to be married forever, until death do us part, and have many children. At least I got that last part right!

My grandparents and my parents were both married forever,

and both had great marriages. My dad still chases my mom around the house, brings her flowers from the garden regularly, and thinks she is the most beautiful woman in the world. Both sets of my grandparents were married past their fiftieth wedding anniversary, and my one grandpa chased grandma around so much that they had fourteen children.

When I learned about sex in my fifth grade sex education class, I can remember thinking, "Holy crap, my grandpa and grandma did that fourteen times . . . gross!" Grandma always said, "We have so many children because grandpa could never keep his hands to himself." I finally understood what that meant, and it made for very uncomfortable Sunday afternoons with my grandparents. Emotional scars aside, I have been beyond blessed to learn about family from the best teachers. From an early age, I was committed to provide for and take care of my family.

Unfortunately, after seventeen years of marriage, I had two titles that were soon going to describe me: former spouse and co-parent. I felt like a failure and I was ashamed. But the hardest part of all was telling the kids that we were getting divorced. To this day, it is the most painfully raw emotion and stress that my body has ever felt. The looks on their faces and their reactions were devastating. That evening, after the kids were tucked in and I was off to my motel, I committed to being a family always and forever, no matter what! I wrote down everything that I was going to do as a father in this situation. I pulled from what I saw my father and my grandfathers do, and I started writing. My finalized list for my family (which includes my ex) included:

- Continue to go to church as a family.
- Eat four nice, sit-down meals a month as a family.
- Continue to have a family Christmas and as many other holidays together as possible.

- ◉ *Never fight with their mom and never say a bad word about her to the kids . . . ever!*
- ◉ *Work hard to continue to financially provide for my family.*

To this day, three years later, I follow these five rules. We are not your typical divorced family. I feel that we are doing much better and making a conscious effort to continue to grow this Oola.

OOLAGURU

The Motorcycle and Man Camp

I was blessed with great parents. My mom taught me how to love and that life is a wonderful adventure to explore. She taught me that we are all equal in God's eyes, no better, no worse. My dad taught me to have confidence in myself, respect others, act in integrity, and to work hard to provide for my family. That last one, to provide, I must have really heard. More later . . .

Growing up, I watched my dad wake up early, come home late, change clothes, and go to his second job. He worked weekends, too. He worked hard to provide for us. He even took a third job on the town board so he could take us on a family vacation each year. He worked hard so my mom could stay home with us. This is the way they liked it. This was the way we liked it. We were far from rich, but we felt as if we were lacking nothing. We felt loved.

My wife is a wonderful mother and spouse. She loves being a mom and wouldn't want to be anywhere else. She is a pro. I may be biased, but I argue it would be tough to find a better mother and wife. She supports me, has patience with my imperfections, and realizes I am always a work in progress.

Early in our marriage, we settled into the traditional roles as modeled by our parents. My wife took care of the kids, and I brought home the paycheck.

Somewhere along the way, through examples, I formed my own idea of what it meant to be the "man of the house." Work hard, provide for the family, drop the check on the table every Friday, and then go into my cave and work on the computer and watch TV only to rest so I could start it all over on Monday.

At that time, none of us thought there was anything wrong with that. As with everything, I had a tugging thought that I could be a better father. The whole motto of the pursuit of Oola is to balance and grow. I felt I could grow as the man of the house. I felt I could step up to another level. The feeling persisted, but since no one was complaining, we continued to roll with it until a fall day just three years ago.

I was driving the kids to school. It's a wonderful Christian school, but it is about twenty-five minutes away. We take a busy highway to get there that is eight lanes across; four in each direction. It was a normal morning with normal conversation. Then we saw it . . .

I must go back. Again, I was the classic provider. In all my self-proclaimed awesomeness, I had this distorted belief that since I was the only one bringing home a paycheck, I could pretty much buy whatever I wanted. I am guy to the core.

If it has a motor, I want it. If it has a big motor, I *really* want it. If it has a big motor and looks cool, I buy it. I had a beautiful custom black chopper. I had progressed up the motorcycle chain over the years and this was my trophy. It sounded tough. When I would fire it up, the rumble echoing off the garage walls and the smell of gasoline would make my body happy from the inside out. It was therapeutic. The bike looked every bit as sick as it sounded. It was a head-turner. I heard the saying once: "Don't love anything that can't love you back." That is probably true, but this bike could challenge that quote.

Back to the ride to school. We were on the highway going highway speed. Countless cars, the slowest ones going sixty-five miles per hour. We look across the highway to the oncoming four lanes. It was in the distance, but it was as if the seas were parting. The mass of rush-hour traffic was abruptly veering to the left and to the right.

Cars, trucks, and semis all pulled to the left and right, leaving the center two lanes void of any cars. In that space, all we could see were sparks. As we got closer, still rolling, end over end, was a crumpled motorcycle. Immediately behind it was a man, sliding down the highway, hands in the air as if trying to stop the traffic from running him over. It all happened in a second; it felt like a year.

Our car was dead silent.

For as long as I can remember, my family had pressured me to sell my bike. I always said no, under the same justification, "I bring home the money, I can buy, and for that matter, do, what I want." I wasn't purposely trying to be selfish.

But I was being selfish. I was only thinking of me. I never truly considered what would happen if that were me on the road that day. I would leave four kids fatherless and one super-sweet gal husbandless.

With the rescue vehicles racing to the scene, my oldest daughter said, "Now, Dad, will you sell your bike?" I didn't say a word. After dropping the kids off, I went home and immediately listed my bike on Craigslist. I listed it for $3,000 under the market value. I wanted to sell it fast before I changed my mind. It sold that night.

Witnessing the motorcycle accident was the event that closed the selfish chapter in my role as husband and father. I was inspired to step out of my default role as traditional provider. I opened my mind to consider the needs of my entire family when making big decisions. I went in search of ways to improve and grow. This pursuit led me to Man Camp.

I was convinced (only slightly against my will) to leave the city and the comforts of my own home and go to Man Camp, a male-only church retreat. Not only did I leave my most basic home comforts (i.e., DVR, Internet, AC, etc.), I was forced to leave my comfort zone relating to my faith.

I try not to be judgmental or, more accurately, prejudgmental. However, I would not be honest if I didn't tell you I had preconceived ideas of what a man at a church camp would look like. I pictured a guy in khaki shorts, black socks, running shoes, tucked-in golf shirt, with a brown belt around a bulging mid-line.

I'm more of a longboard, chopper beach bike, T-shirt, ball cap, flip-flops kind of guy. I didn't think I would fit in. Not only did I have a preconceived visual image, I also had preconceived expectations about personalities. I expected to meet a bunch of Bible-thumping, socially awkward Urkels with whom I would have no compatibility.

I am not too proud to admit when I am wrong—and I was wrong. Totally wrong.

What I met at Man Camp were men, real men. Not men as culture would have us aspire to, but authentic men who care about their faith, their wives, their children, their communities, and the legacies they will leave.

At Man Camp I learned three things:

1) **Real men are humble.**
   This doesn't mean weak. In fact, it is confidence, but a quiet confidence. It means not taking credit for the good. It means helping shoulder the blame. Man stuff. It does exist; I saw it in men at Man Camp.

2) **Real men forgive.**
   They forgive those who have hurt them, and, just as important, they forgive themselves for their own shortcomings and failures.

3) **Real men work to leave a legacy.**
   In my classic provider days, when I thought about leaving something for my family, it was in the form of money (i.e., a will). The men at Man Camp desire to leave something deeper and more noble. They invest their time and energy into the next generation of men, passing on core values, morals, and ethics to create strong, next-generation men.

What I learned at Man Camp was what is required to be an authentic man. Camp permanently changed my definition of a man. I met men who are the spiritual leaders of their families. It was cool, and I wanted that. I realized that up to that point I had failed as spiritual leader of my family, and it became clear that I needed to improve. Since my eighteen-year-old son went up that mountain with me and wants to go back next year, I guess I'm on the right track.

OOLAFAMILY TIPS:

1) **Love**

Love is beautiful and a requirement for the OolaLife. Give love, receive love. Forgive when hurt. Accept forgiveness when presented. Let go when necessary, such as when your kids leave home to make their own way. Make sure the love is pure, without conditions or layered in dysfunction. Pure love propels you toward Oola; toxic love blocks your way.

2) **Lead**

Regardless of your role in your family, lead by example. Lead in a way that inspires others do better and be better. There is great responsibility in a leadership role, but also great reward.

3) **Commit**

Commit to your family. Don't let life happen to you. Be active and engaged in family activities. Healthy family relationships propel you toward Oola. Toxic family relationships block the way. If you invest and take an active role in your family, you will invest in the life of your dreams.

OOLAFIELD

Love It or Leave It

"The best career advice I've gotten
is to stay focused, keep moving forward."

—Tyga

OolaField is your career, your vocation in life. Most people spend one-third of their time during their working years devoted to this. If you are a stay-at-home parent, it is more like 100 percent.

There are two categories in OolaField: 1) a day job, and 2) a dream job. Most of us have a day job. Many of us aspire to our dream job. Some are lucky enough to get there.

A day job is typically something you have to do to make ends meet. It is not your passion, but it pays the bills.

Your dream job is what you aspire to. If money were no object, what would you like to do? What do you feel called to do? For some of you that is to start your own business, be a writer, stay at home with the kids, be a doctor, even become a firefighter.

Jon Acuff, in his bestselling book *Quitter,* taps into the tension many of us feel between our day job and our dream job—that gap between what you *have* to do and what you'd *love* to do. He encourages you to quit your day job to follow your dream, but with one required component—a plan.

We have known many people who have quit their day jobs in a moment of frustration to pursue their dream job with no plan to bridge the gap. Bad plan.

It is very Oola to pursue what you love. But hear us on these three points: 1) figure out what you would like to do, and 2) then figure out a way to get paid to do it, then 3) formulate a plan for the transition. Caution: Don't make the leap from your day job to your dream job until you have a solid plan for the transition, otherwise you will put serious strain on the other F's of Oola.

If you see no way out, or if you're content in your day job, no worries. There is great honor in honest work. And if you're going to do it, do it with style.

There is an old fable of the three stonecutters. As the story goes, the three men were working in a rock quarry cutting stone. On one particular day, a visitor to the rock quarry walked up to the first stonecutter and said, "What are you doing?"

The first stonecutter got a frustrated look on his face and said, "What do you mean, what am I doing? Can't you see what I am doing? I cut stone. I get here at 7 a.m. and leave at 6 p.m. and all day long I take this pick and I cut stone."

The guest walked up to the second stonecutter and said, "Hey, can I ask you a question? What are you doing?"

The second stonecutter wiped the sweat off his brow and replied, "You want to know what I am doing? I'm paying my bills. That's what I'm doing. I've got hungry mouths to feed, a mortgage to pay, clothes to buy. I am here to pay the bills."

The guest walked up to the third stonecutter and said, "Can I ask you a question? What are you doing?"

The third stonecutter likewise wiped the sweat off his brow, picked up his pick, and pointed it off into the distance where they were constructing a building. "You want to know what I'm doing? I'm helping to build that cathedral." With a subtle smile and twinkle in his eye he continued, "It will be in that building where the bishop will come, and he will teach us all he knows, and lives will be transformed." He paused and said, "You want to know what I'm doing? I'm changing lives for generations to come."

Pursuing your dream job (with a plan) is very Oola. And if that is not your path, do honest work with style, like the third stonecutter. That is Oola as well.

Serve others in your field and you will be served.

OOLASEEKER

Game Changers

Life is packed full of so many memories and experiences that they are impossible to count. But I have heard that at the end of your life there will only be three major events that truly change the course of your life and define your existence. These events can be positive or negative. They were usually precipitated by a choice made at a fork in the road or by chance circumstances. For instance, you get a promotion, but you have to move out of the country. You choose to move, which leads to meeting the love of your life, getting married, having kids, and everything that goes along with starting a family and setting up a new life. Everyone you meet, the coffee shops you frequent, the happy days and the sad days, are all a result of your decision to move. Then one day, years down the road, you get in a car accident that leaves you paralyzed. Now a major event or circumstance has created a new life-changing event that will alter your future and create a new design for your life.

Many of my stories in this book will discuss the time that I was at the bottom—the time I made the phone call to the OolaGuru. There are two reasons that I will spend extra ink on this section of my life. The first reason is that I feel many of you are reading this book because you want something better for your life, and I want to show you that no matter where you are, you not only deserve an OolaLife but you also have the ability to go get it.

The second reason is that one of my life-changing events occurred that night at the motel when I reached out to the OolaGuru, an event that has changed the course of my life forever and has brought Oola back within my grasp. As I write and reflect,

I play out the coincidences that have led me to this lake cabin in northern Minnesota.

The fireplace pulls the chill out of the air and the soothing call of loons seems to synchronize with the music of Tyrone Wells in the background. "I'm not a writer. Am I?" Looking at my cup of coffee and my computer screen filled with words, it appears I am. It's all a bit surreal.

I think deep into the coincidences. Why did that guy get arrested? If I had chosen a different motel, would I still be at the bottom? Have I ever previously and coincidentally run into that guy who got arrested, at a gas station, restaurant, or maybe even at my business? All I know is that the dramatic scene of officers yelling, the thud of a door being rammed open, and police lights penetrating the cheap curtains right into my sleeping eyes woke me and triggered my brain to instantly change direction

> **Following your passion and turning your passion into your career is more possible now than at any other time in history.**

and take action. I wish I could thank the guy who got arrested that night for being part of a positive life-changing event for me. And now, maybe, for you.

The twenty-four hours after the phone call was like a "dog years" thing. Time seemed to pass in years, not hours. I put into action a plan that, though very difficult at the time, brought me to this place—a place where life is more balanced and growing. The morning after The Call I drove up into the mountains and I got real with my situation. I drew my own OolaWheel (which you will learn about in Chapter 24) in a light brown, leather-bound notebook and filled it out honestly. I was all two's and three's (which is bad) and I remember thinking, "Well, at least I'm balanced."

Once I felt solid about where I was, I went on to my OolaPlan (Chapter 25) and my OolaPath (Chapter 26). After a long morning, I was done, and there it was: a plan written on paper describing exactly what I had to do to get my OolaLife back. At that moment I said out loud (and with a sarcastic tone), "If this works, I will dedicate my life to educating and enlightening the world on Oola." Long story short, it started to work, and I slowly shifted my career toward working full-time with Oola.

Following your passion and turning it into your career is more possible now than at any other time in history. For example, let's say you live an average life in a city of a million people, and your secret passion is orchids. You can't wait to get home from work so you can work with your orchids. You read about them and figure out better ways to grow and care for them. It's what you think about and it's what you would love to dedicate your life to. Now let's go back fifteen years ago. To quit your day job and pursue a life of orchids, you would need to rent some space, build the perfect orchid shop in the perfect location, and put serious money into branding and marketing your orchid shop. Your reach would be roughly a three-to five-mile radius and there would be three people in that market who love orchids as much as you do, and one of them would be your sister. The reality would set in that you have to sell a lot of orchids to keep the lights on, and you would either need to close the doors or diversify.

Technology today makes the world smaller, and therefore the opportunities are endless. Today, your market is no longer the three-to five-mile ring that surrounds your orchid shop—your market is the world. Your market is anyone with Internet and a computer or a smartphone—and that's a lot of people. You can blog about your love for orchids, you can share about them on your orchid Facebook page, find others who love orchids on Twitter, and you can sell orchids all over the world, not simply to make money, but because you really love them.

You think this example is far-fetched? It isn't. This is an actual example of a real guy who really loves orchids and now makes a living sharing his love of orchids to the world. The orchid guy and I have similar paths when it comes to OolaField. I worked at my career very hard every day, and then after the kids went to bed I tapped into my true passion, Oola.

I started developing a plan to take Oola to the world . . . basically to start an OolaRevolution! It was a slow and sleep-deprived two years but by the end of that time a business was born. People were wearing Oola hats and T-shirts, corporations were being taught Oola principles in the workplace, and companies were approaching us to license Oola for their lifestyle products. What started as a word and a personal passion had evolved into a multi-million dollar lifestyle business.

I am reluctantly going to share my personal mission statement that I entered into my cell phone two years ago and read every morning and every night. Only four people have seen the following words prior to this book. This mission statement was written in the "Be. Do. Have." format. Basically, what I want to be, what I need to do, and what I will have once completed.

BE. A visionary leader, educator, entertainer, and facilitator of Oola around the world.

DO. Forever be grateful for all the experiences along my journey—past, present, and future. Forever make choices based on love, integrity, and the constant pursuit of achieving my life's purpose. Forever be certain that I already possess all the knowledge and wisdom needed to create this home of Oola and bring the opportunity of the OolaLife to everyone.

HAVE. *The opportunity for myself and my children to stand on every country in the world and experience the inspiration of God.*

This simple mission statement got me through many endless nights of work. It helped me make difficult decisions to keep the company going in the right direction. It gave me the courage to sell my business and take the well-planned and well-thought-out jump to full-time Oola, and one step closer to my OolaLife!

OOLAGURU

A Place Unknown

I have had both day jobs and dream jobs and even one that fell somewhere between the two.

I've had plenty of day jobs. Delivery guy, hotel gift-shop clerk, assembly line worker, just to name a few. Some I liked, some I tolerated, and some I couldn't wait to leave. I always tried to do my best because I believe there is honor in honest work, and because I knew they were stepping stones to something else, something bigger, something better.

For seventeen years, I owned my own business in my hometown. I loved it. I got to know lots of great and interesting people; many are still close friends today. What I realized about myself through these years is that my dream job is to help people.

I enjoy helping people. I also love creating, building, and growing. It was fun to build a business and watch it grow. As time went on I grew tired of the paperwork. Each year there would be more and more of it. When it got to the point where I was spending more time on the paperwork than with the people, it was time to move on. This is when I closed the chapter on my job that fell between day job and dream job.

I don't live in a box well. I have a natural itch for adventure. What you seek you find. In 1999, I had the opportunity to open up a branch of my business—my day job—in Dubai and share it with that part of the world. This tapped right into my value system of wanting to share what I know with other people.

With this opportunity, instead of impacting one person at a time, I had a chance to impact an entire region. This was in 1999, before

Dubai was even on the map, and it was cool . . . this was right up my alley. I still am involved in this project today.

Despite how cool the adventure was, as our kids got older we realized we missed our families and wanted to educate our kids in the States. So we returned home, where I still owned my U.S. business. When we moved back, though, I realized the paperwork in my business had increased even more. Gratefully, we were financially secure and we evaluated our options.

My wife and I attended a wedding reception and sat at a table with my niece and her husband, who had traveled from Phoenix to attend the event. They talked about how low the home prices were in their area. This was in 2008, the pit of the great recession. I like real estate, and have dabbled in it over the years, so I just thought she didn't know what she was talking about. Being from the Midwest, and always looking for ways to escape the winters, I had looked at real estate in Phoenix a few years earlier. It had been unaffordable for us.

But, after the wedding reception, it only took me ten minutes of Googling to reveal my niece was right. I was on flight a few days later.

We have a pretty simple financial guide—if we have enough money saved, we can consider buying something. If not, it is not for us. We will have to wait until we've saved up or we'll have to pass.

This trip, though, was crazy. Houses that were $1,000,000 just two years earlier were now $350,000. I took it as a sign. So, on the way back to the airport to head home, I made a ridiculously low cash offer on a fully furnished house. I had no expectation that they would accept. Heck, this was supposed to be a recon/ information-seeking trip only. My wife and kids hadn't even seen the house yet.

The sellers accepted my offer. I guess we were moving. In a typical example of my family's awesome and unconditional support, they were onboard.

I sold my business and we moved.

So this was it! I had arrived. Forty-two years old, fully retired, not a worry in the world. I played golf, traveled, ran, went out to eat. The American Dream realized!

Sounds awesome, huh? It was . . . for a while. It's not that I was unhappy; life was good. But I didn't feel balanced. My OolaField was low. How low? The summer after I sold my business, I was sitting on the dock reading Tim Ferriss's bestseller, titled *The 4-Hour Workweek*. My brother pulled up, glanced at the book title, and said, with his consistent sarcasm, "Planning on working more?"

I needed more purpose in work. I needed to use my skills for the benefit of others . . . somehow.

Since 1997, on and off, a group of us have met annually for our OolaPlanning meeting, during which we map out our personal long-term strategies.

That winter, we met in Vegas. That was when the OolaSeeker pulled me aside. He had been getting his Oola back for some time now and I was super excited to hear about his wins and to see the principles working . . . again. He pitched me on sharing what we know with the world. He had me at "Hello."

You see, there is a deep desire in all of us—our life's purpose. My life experiences have taught me that my dream job is to create, build, and grow. And, professionally, I am most fulfilled if I am doing this for large quantities of people in the category of greatest interest to me—helping others balance and grow their life and helping the world pursue Oola. I know that because when I share this with others I am inspired. I have extra energy. It's as if time is suspended.

I still like to run, golf, and travel. But that day in Vegas with the OolaSeeker reconnected me with my dream job, and that is to help the world discover the OolaLife . . . but in board shorts and flip-flops, anonymously, from a place unknown.

OOLAFIELD TIPS:

1) **Love It or Leave It**

There is great nobility in honest work. If you work at a job, be grateful for employment and do it with style or leave. Who knows? Your efforts may be noticed and you may move up the chain. If your day job is completely unfulfilling and only a stepping stone to your dream job, that is fine. We encourage you to pursue your dream job, but with a plan. Do not make the leap until you bridge the financial gap.

2) **Stay Relevant**

Times change, and jobs change. To advance, you must stay current. Skate to where the puck is going, not to where it is. Whether in your day job or toward your dream job, look ahead.

Read, find a mentor, network, learn, and grow. This will keep you more secure in your current position and will open up new opportunities.

3) **Serve**

Whatever you do, take it from a perspective of service to others. Think of the fable of the three stonecutters. They had the exact same job, with completely different perspectives. All three men received the same paycheck, but the stonecutter with a vision that he was changing lives and serving others went home feeling a lot more fulfilled at the end of each day. Be the third stonecutter.

OOLAFAITH

It's Not All About You

"Faith is taking the first step even when you don't see the whole staircase."

—Martin Luther King, Jr.

Faith is defined as a complete trust or confidence in someone or something. A strong belief in God or in the doctrines of a religion, based on spiritual apprehension rather than proof. Faith is your purpose in life. How you see your place in this world is something you need to explore to attain Oola.

We were taught that two topics will divide a room: 1) politics and 2) faith. This book will not speak of politics (because the topic bores us, and it is possible to get the OolaLife without politics), but we are not going to shy away from faith. Understanding your place in this world is necessary for a life that is balanced and growing.

OOLASEEKER

The Struggle

With all my heart, I have always believed that the purpose of my life is designed by God. I have no problem having the faith to put my life in God's hands, and I am very grateful that I have this

> **It is human nature to overthink our lives, our decisions, and our purpose.**

understanding within my heart. But when it comes to trusting my faith, I have the tendency to go inside my head and then start questioning everything. I think that it is human nature to overthink our lives, our decisions, and our purpose. I heard a story a couple of years ago that best describes how to bridge the heart and head thing. The story goes something like this:

A university professor asked this question: "Did God create every-thing that exists?"

Many students replied, "Yes, God did create everything that exists."

The next question the professor asked was, "If God created everything, then you are saying that God created evil, since evil exists. And according to the principle that our work defines who we are, then God is evil." The auditorium was silent.

Eventually, a student raised his hand and said, "Professor, I want to ask you a question. Does cold exist?"

The professor replied, "What kind of question is this? Of course cold exists."

The young man replied, "In fact, sir, cold does not exist. According to the laws of physics, what we perceive as cold is actually the absence of heat. Absolute zero (-460 degrees Fahrenheit) is the total

absence of heat; all matter becomes inert and incapable of reaction at that temperature. Cold does not exist. We have created this
word to describe how we feel if we don't have enough heat."

The student asked another question, "Professor, does darkness
exist?"

The professor responded, "Yes, of course it does."

The student replied, "You are wrong again, sir. Darkness in reality
is the absence of light. Light we can study, but not darkness. We can
measure light, but we cannot measure darkness. How can you know
how dark a certain space is? You measure the amount of light present. Darkness is a term used by man to describe what happens when
there is no light present. So professor I ask you, does evil exist?"

Now uncertain, the professor responded, "Of course evil exists.
I see it every day. Murders, wars, crimes, and simply man's inhuman-
ity to man prove that evil exists. These manifestations are nothing
but evil."

The student interrupted, "Evil does not exist, sir. Evil is simply the
absence of God. It is just like the darkness and the cold. Simply, a
word that man has created to describe the absence of God. God
did not create evil. Evil is not like faith, or love, that do exist just as
does light and heat. Evil is the result of what happens when man
does not have faith that God's love is present in his heart. It's like the
cold that shows up in the absence of heat and the darkness that
shows up in the absence of light."

The story ends with the professor being stumped and bewildered,
and the claim is that the student was Albert Einstein.

Whether it's true or not, this very simple story reminds me to have
faith in my heart because it is impossible to figure it out in my head.
I continue to work hard with my faith and I have committed to
always improving this key area of my life.

OOLAGURU

Finishing Strong

In my bio, under the category OolaFaith, I list, "Not yet the man I want to be, but thank God I am not the man I used to be." That perfectly summarizes where I am on my personal journey regarding my faith. As a young guy coming up, the ride was fast. It was exciting and fun. College, marriage, career, kids, travel—those were exciting times. I was grateful for all the good flowing my way, but I was grateful to . . . me. I had a humble exterior, but inside I was taking all the credit. I was racing toward all the material targets as set by society and myself. The race was fun, fast, and extreme. I had many amazing and big moments. The problem was, I was so focused on the big moments that I missed the little ones—the occasional performance, conferences, and even a birthday. I was pretty good, but I could have done better.

I justified my absence, either physical or mental, because I felt like I was succeeding in my role as provider. I was bringing home a fat paycheck.

My wife is amazing. And she gets smarter every year. Actually, her intelligence is consistent, but my awareness and appreciation of her wisdom deepens daily. I was busy bringing home the paychecks and she would keep the home in check. She did it willingly, lovingly, and with little outside recognition. I was the one in the limelight. She was the one holding it all together, with a smile on her face the entire time.

I would have my ups and downs. She would remain steady. When asked, she would let anyone know that her foundation was God. In my younger years, I would nod and smile in support, but inside almost giggle. "Really? You have that much faith?"

Through my fake smile, I felt like my way was the right way, and her way was just . . . cute. I continued to buy cool stuff, have cool experiences, and meet cool people. While she, home with the kids, seemed more sincerely content with life. My life was good, but if I wanted to continue my quest to balance and grow, I knew I needed to explore faith. I felt there was something missing. My Oola was good, but could have been better. Faith was, and quite frankly is, my wobbly plate. I had been introduced to God from time to time, but never took the time to get to know Him. Faith clearly was the F of Oola I needed to work on most. It has demanded most of my focus over the past five years.

All I can say from my own personal experience is that, as I continue to grow in faith, I feel way more content and have a clearer understanding of my purpose in this world. In short, I feel small . . . but in a good way.

Regarding my personal faith journey. I don't feel like I started strong, but I am committed to finishing strong. Oh, by the way, I don't miss any of those little moments any more.

OOLAFAITH TIPS:

1) **Don't Wait**

   Don't be closed-minded on the topic of faith. Listen to others, learn, explore the topic. Don't wait until confronted with a major life crisis to search for the "why" in life. Humble yourself to the point where you are open to the idea that others may have something to teach you on the subject.

2) **Plug In**

   Whether your heart tells you to find a church, spiritual community, a blog, a book, or a small group of others like you who want to work on increasing their faith, get involved. Plug into whatever feels right to you.

3) **Give**

   Nothing is more Oola than giving. As you explore your faith and plug into a community, find a place to give. It doesn't have to be money; it can be giving of your time or your talent. By giving, with no conditions, you will get a glimpse of the good in this world. If you give purely, it is nearly impossible to not grow in faith.

OOLAFRIENDS

Virtual or Real . . . Choose Wisely

*"A true friend is someone who lets you have
the total freedom to be yourself."*

— Jim Morrison

OolaFriends includes two categories: friends and acquaintances. Friends are your true friends. People you open up to and share with. True friends are composed of the collection of key non-family relationships that you have built over the years.

True friendships withstand the test of time. With true friends, you have seen their good and bad qualities, and they have seen the same in you, and you choose to stay friends through it all. True friendships are valued, deep, and enduring.

Acquaintances are necessary and cool. They are typically greater in number and less in meaning. They are all the people in your life that you are not related to but that you interact with. They could be classmates, coworkers, teammates, neighbors, Facebook friends, or Twitter followers. These relationships tend to be a bit more superficial and connected by a mutual interest or forced interaction.

Growing your OolaFriends does not necessarily mean in quantity. Quantity may be a component, but quality may be what is needed as well. It is valuable as you pursue a life in Oola to expand and improve your friend base. It is nice to have a group of people outside your family as a resource, whether it be to open up to, network with, or just have fun.

OOLASEEKER

My Zebra-Striped Bikini Underwear

Hopefully, every one of you has seen the movies Stand by Me, The Sandlot, *and* The Goonies. *If not, put this book down and run, don't walk, to the nearest library, rental kiosk, or online streaming service.*

These are classic movies about the deep connections and memories created by experiencing life with true friends. I have many virtual friends and acquaintances, but it is the couple of people that I have been friends with forever who have created the cinematic-type experiences that bring a smile to my face twenty years later.

I am not sure what stressed me out more at this point—that I had a gun in my face, or that I was just asked to get out of the car and stand along the interstate wearing nothing but zebra-striped, bikini-cut underwear.

I could literally write a book just on the topic of friendship. I am not sure if I would want my kids to read it, but I promise it would be an international bestseller. My closest friend of all time would be in half the chapters. This guy inspired me to shoot out the windows of my parents' chicken coop in elementary school, get involved in numerous bottlerocket fights with the city kids in middle school, cut the roof off my dad's Ford Galaxy 500 in high school, and take a sledgehammer to a wall in college to find a place to hide our beer.

He then went on to more noble tasks of becoming the best man in my wedding and the godfather to my fourth child. He was contemplating becoming a Catholic priest before he met his beautiful wife and started a family. I always thought he would have to dedicate the rest of his life to priesthood just to have a chance to get into heaven for all the crap he pulled growing up, but he has become an amazing husband, a fantastic father, and remains a great friend.

If you are a screenplay writer, pay attention—your future Academy Award exists in what you are about to read next.

It was the summer of 1989, and Chris and I were rolling through our little town of 800 people in his cherry red 1978 Chevy Monte Carlo. The back end was slightly jacked up, the rims were chromed out, and the purposely created hole in the muffler gave it the "rough and tough" sound needed to create the effect of a real badass car. The vibrations of AC/DC echoed throughout the car and you can guarantee that my Oklahoma Sooners hat was on backwards.

We were discussing how lame this town was and how crazy it was that the city's annual fireworks display had been canceled due to the drought and the risk of wildfires. Neither one of us had really ever been out of North Dakota physically, but mentally we owned the world and thought that this town was the worst place to be at that given moment.

As we rolled a few miles down the road, we saw our buddy Mark chilling in his car listening to music. He was the guy with all the cool cases of cassette tapes. He must have had three or four large, double-sided containers the size of small suitcases that held hundreds of tapes, which provided unlimited music possibilities. I only had three cassette tapes to my name: AC/DC's Back in Black, Bon Jovi's Slippery When Wet, and Poison's Look What the Cat Dragged In (which my dad tried to throw away because they "looked like four long-haired girls" on the cover).

When we pulled up to Mark's car, we noticed that he didn't look good. Was it possible that Mark was crying? Yep, he was. We weren't sure if we were going to make fun of him or take him in and see what was up. We chose to take the high road and invite him *into the jacked-up Monte Carlo. He told us that his longtime girlfriend had broken up with him. He was devastated, and I would have been, too—she was pretty hot for a small-town girl. Two clear options presented themselves. Option one: Drop Mark off as soon as possible and seek out his now ex-girlfriend. (Don't judge, like I said, it was a small town; not a lot of options, and I wasn't related to this girl.) Or, option two: Road trip!*

After weighing our choices for a few minutes, we made a decision. Road trip! The first item on the agenda was simple: north, south, east, or west. Not a destination, just a direction. The unanimous decision was to head south and see where the road led us. We could have chosen east, which would have taken us through the Land of 10,000 Lakes, to the home of the Bears and the White Sox, through the Big Apple, and to the narrow streets of Boston. We could have chosen west and trekked through Big Sky territory, the Rockies, the Golden Gate Bridge, and the grandeur of the West Coast. Heading north was quickly eliminated, since we would have been in Canada in less than four hours. Little did we know that heading south was pretty much a thousand miles of wheat fields before we'd see anything remotely different than our own backyard!

We then proceeded to do what every responsible but inexperienced traveler would do. We left notes for our parents to let them know that we would be gone for a while, borrowed Chris's dad's gas card, and loaded a cooler with a couple loaves of bread, endless amounts of sandwich meat, and Mark's nunchucks for safety. The plan went from concept to on the road in less than an hour. We pointed the car south and we were off.

There are three distinct parts of this trip that we talk about every time we see each other: Steelheart, the Oklahoma Sooners stadium, and the zebra-striped bikini underwear. We drove all night and we were somewhere in Nebraska or Kansas, most likely near a wheat field. Chris and I were riding in the front and Mark was sleeping in the back. We decided it was time for him to wake up. It was our method of waking him up, though, that was cruel. While driving, we found a very poorly dubbed copy of the Steelheart's song "I'll Never Let You Go (Angel Eyes)." So we made a bet to see how many times we could play that song over and over before Mark was reminded of his long-lost, hot girlfriend and he would wake up and start to cry.

I guessed seven; Chris guessed five. The final number was three. Once the song started for the third time, the back seat became the fourth of July fireworks we were seeking. His words said it all: "For the love of God, would you please turn this off!" We started laughing hysterically, and a couple minutes later Mark was laughing right there with us. I guess it is nice to have friends comfort you when you are feeling down, but then push you to move on and not enable you to remain depressed over something out of your control. Good lesson learned.

As the journey continued, the endless sea of wheat fields accompanied our talks on life—what we wanted to become and what we wanted to do over the next couple of years and beyond. The conversations were deep at times and at other times just superficial bull crap. The quiet times were few and far between, but they provided moments to reflect on what lay behind us and what lay ahead of us. And one thing that lay ahead of us was the stadium for the Oklahoma Sooners in Norman, Oklahoma.

We now had our first destination.

I had been a fan of the Oklahoma Sooners ever since I bought a maroon cap that matched my maroon Adidas sneakers. It's a weird way to pick a college football team, but the cap was pretty damn cool. It was my signature piece of clothing and I wore it pretty much every day. Little did I know that those shoes would lead to that cap, which would eventually lead to me climbing a fifteen-foot fence in

Norman, Oklahoma, to play catch on the field at Sooner stadium. The experience was surreal.

It was the first time that I'd ever been in a college sports stadium and it seemed incredibly huge. Chris, Mark, and I were teammates on a high school playoff football team, and to hang out on this field and throw the ball around was one of the cooler experiences of my life. Memories!

Well, we made it this far, we might as well go to Texas. So, we turned the car south and kept rolling down the highway. Dallas and Houston were soon in our rearview mirror and we were moments away from seeing the largest body of water that any of us had ever seen. The Gulf of Mexico, just outside of Galveston, Texas, is nothing to write home about, but I did. I sat on the beach and wrote a letter to my parents thanking them for everything they had done for me and exclaiming my desire to travel the world. The other not so cool thing about Galveston, Texas, is that it's a long drive back to North Dakota. With the Monte now facing north we started to eat up the road on our journey home.

Somewhere in the middle of Texas in the middle of July, the air conditioner in the Monte decided to retire. I remember that it was midnight and still in the upper 90s. Although Chris exclaimed that he now had the air conditioner set at "280" (which meant two windows down and 80 miles per hour), I was still roasting in the back seat. I decided that I'd had enough, and proceeded to strip down to my underwear—my zebra-striped, bikini-cut underwear that I'd gotten as a gag birthday gift from my sisters a month earlier. Gag gift to them, amazing style and comfort to me. As the heat continued to wear on us, Chris decided to set the air conditioner to "290." A couple hours down the road, I was sound asleep from the fatigue of travel when I awoke to the Texas Highway Patrol pulling us over for having our "air conditioner" set too high.

Our only experience with law enforcement up to this point was our local city cop, who played city league softball with us every Thursday night. These officers were different. They were more like the battering ram officers than the softball-playing officers. When they came up to the side of the car, one on the passenger side and one on the driver's side, Chris reached under the seat to grab his wallet. Obviously, not a great move. Before we knew what Chris had done wrong, we had guns pointed at our heads with officers screaming, "Get your hands up where we can see them! Get them up! Get them up!" The officers proceeded to open the car doors and tell us to get out of the car. I am not sure what stressed me out more at this point—that I had a gun in my face, or that I was just asked to get out of the car and stand along the interstate wearing nothing but zebra-striped, bikini-cut underwear. I very politely asked the officer to please allow me to put my jeans on, but soon enough I was half naked on the side of the highway. There we stood, watching the officers ransack the car and pull everything out of the trunk and onto the road.

The whole time they were tearing the car apart, Mark kept whispering to us, "Oh my God, they are going to find my nunchucks." All I remember thinking was, "Holy crap Mark, if nunchucks are illegal in the South, why the hell did you bring them?" It's not like we were smuggling arms across the border for the local Ninja warriors.

Moments later, the officers got in their cars and took off. We repacked all our stuff, including the legal nunchucks, and got back on the road with the car heading north. Right now on my bucket list is to redo this trip with Chris and Mark someday. We would send text messages to the kids to let them know that we will be gone for a while, take our debit cards for gas, eat at every great restaurant along the way, and pack Mark's nunchucks for safety.

OOLAGURU

Stories of Legend

Having been on this planet a while, I have had a ton of friends. Most are acquaintances, neighbors, coworkers, and some that are, let's just say, networked. These acquaintances have resulted in some ridiculous life experiences. Trips in private 747s, private helicopters . . . real VIP stuff.

As cool as all those experiences are, without a doubt, I value my true friendships the most. The ones that have stood the test of time. Three such friends immediately come to mind: one from elementary school, one from high school, and one from college.

Over time, with our families and careers, distance has come between us. The cool thing about friends like these guys is that I could talk to them once a day or once a year, and it wouldn't be too much or too little. Their friendship is consistent. Their friendship is stable. Their friendship is true.

Recently we decided to reunite. We picked a remote island and planned a week. The scenery was beautiful and the beer cold, but the conversation dominated the trip.

We shared a ton of laughs, mostly reminiscing and laughing at ourselves, like when, in high school, Seeg got to the taco stand counter and his bill was $3.18 and he asked me for eighteen cents. I gave it to him, and he replied, "Thanks, I didn't want to have to break a quarter."

Or when my mom dressed me in a "cute" purple short/tank top combo for the first day of kindergarten. When the teacher lined up the boys and girls in separate lines for bathroom time, she put me in the girls' line. I did everything short of giving her a glimpse of my junk to get in the correct line.

Or when Dale landed in the Middle East, hopped in a taxi, and when the driver asked him if it was his first time to the region, he responded, "*Si.*" It was at this point he realized there were more than two languages in the world.

Or when Ern, while out for a night with the boys, stole a mutual friend's phone, fired up the camera, and . . . enough said.

These are the stories of legend. These guys are worthy of legend. We encourage each other, learn from each other, keep each other in check, support each other, and grow old with each other. We have each other's backs, even when we don't speak in months. It's nice to have a group of true friends, outside of family, who clearly have no agenda, other than just to hang and enjoy each other's company. Invest time in the friendships you value most, they are necessary if you desire an OolaLife.

OOLAFRIENDS TIPS:

1) **Stay Connected**

   With the Internet and all the social media available, it has never been easier to stay connected. Take advantage of this cool technology to do just that.

2) **Share**

   Use your friends as a resource. Learn from their experiences. Take it deeper. Be vulnerable and open up. A support system outside your family is very valuable. True friends want what is best for you and want to see you win.

3) **Go Old School**

   Even with all the cool technology to connect us, don't forget to invest in quality time with friends. Log some face time—the real kind, not just the Apple kind. Pick up the phone and actually talk, don't just text. Book a trip and reconnect and reminisce. It is soothing for the soul. It is Oola.

OOLAFUN

The Spice of Life

"Just play. Have fun. Enjoy the game."

—Michael Jordan

OolaFun is whatever activity or hobby you are personally passionate about. Unlike many of the other 7 F's of Oola, this category is very unique to you, and is very much driven by your personality. It may be a craft, reading, golf, cars, photography, travel, surfing, gardening, fishing, skateboarding, writing, tennis, antiques . . . the list is endless.

Your OolaFun is also an easy category to identify. It is usually what you do on that one day when you can do whatever you want. It's what's fun to you. It's subjective. It doesn't even need to be a hobby or a sport. It can be a simple as a sunset or a cup of coffee by a fire. No need to elaborate.

OOLASEEKER

My Ten-Mile Circle

Fun is a very interesting F for me to talk about. I really wish I could dazzle you, and myself, with some cool, exotic stories of adventure and discovery of a lost world. But, I can't . . . yet! Ninety-nine percent of my childhood existed in a ten-mile circle surrounding the farm where I grew up. The school I went to was six miles from the front door heading east.

My grandparents' farm was about nine miles straight south and we would visit them many Sundays. The land we worked and the place we went to fix any farm machinery was about six miles west of the farm. I have no idea why we never drove north, but it felt like it was off-limits. It wasn't, but I was just a kid, and that's how it seemed to me.

Once a year, we would make a trip to the big city to get all the back-to-school stuff we needed for the year. The trip felt like forever. We would take blankets and pillows to ease the stress from the drive.

I believe everyone has something they can teach me to make me better.

My mom would pack sandwiches so that we would only have to eat out once. My dad would check the oil and fill the gas tank of the Ford Econ-ovan. My sisters would be in their best shopping attire from the year before and we would all load into the car. Mom and dad sat in the front, and the rest of us were left to fend for the best window seat available. An hour later, we were pulling into the city and, even though it was a city of only 50,000, it felt huge to me.

Looking back, all of this seems ridiculous. Nowadays, I drive more than an hour every day just getting my kids to school, picking them back up, and getting them dropped off at their soccer practices and back home. We drive six to eight hours just for a fun weekend, normally by picking a direction: north, south, east, or west (I learned this from a couple of friends of mine).

As ridiculously simple as my childhood sounds, it taught me two very valuable lessons. Lesson one: I have a deep desire to see the world, venture out, and explore everything. I have this childish side of me that, when I travel, I actually feel like an explorer: hiking, biking, driving, or boating to find some new place or undiscovered treasures. The difference between myself and my childhood adventure idols (Captain Kangaroo, the Mutual of Omaha Wild Kingdom guy, and Jacques Cousteau) is that I drag along my five kids, carry about five cells phones, eat out every meal, never hang with wild animals, and stay at nice hotels.

Lesson two: I learned from a very early age that, for me, fun is simple and usually surrounded by family. I can honestly say that there has almost never been a day when I didn't have fun. I have the innate ability to have fun doing almost anything. Simply because, growing up, we had to find fun. You couldn't buy a ticket for fun inside my ten-mile circle. I would build forts with my friends, climb trees, play driveway basketball on an eight-foot rim (I was awesome and I made every game-winning shot—you know, the "3 . . . 2 . . . 1" shots), play endless hours of kick the can with my sisters, and just hang out in the backyard at night to see the most amazing view of the stars ever.

I wanted to know if this trait of having simple fun and the love for adventure was hereditary or at least contagious, so I asked my kids to tell me their ten most memorable fun experiences. They answered:

- Family soccer trips and the weird things we do on them (like stealing oranges from the orchards in Arizona, cruising to the ocean in Florida, and learning to surf in Hawaii, to name a few).

- Rocking to music in the car. Bieber fever was a little difficult to get through, but I managed.
- Impromptu football games. My girls can catch an over-the-head pass at the tail end of a chair pattern forty yards deep. I told them that this will get some random guy to propose to them someday. They already have also been coached to respond with a "No, thank you."
- Driving up in the mountains and parking the car in a snow storm to watch a movie while we all piled in the back seat.
- Shark, Breakout, 3, 2, 1, and Slamhugs—homemade games that we invented.
- German dumpling soup and the Sunday NFL ticket.
- Random trips in random directions with no planning.
- Backyard soccer games to the death.
- Boating down the river.
- Our ten-day drive from Paris to Nice, France.

Most of their responses are anything but glamorous, but they were fun times. It is crazy how much fun we had by being extremely spontaneous, and all but two are easy on the finances.

We have played more football, Frisbee, volleyball, and soccer games than I can count. We have taken long weekends and driven in many different directions to always have some cool theme set the tone for the entire trip. We have camped and roughed it and stayed at five-star hotels. We have found incredible restaurants and tried to grill steaks over a campfire (we burnt the steak, but our dog Dexter ate ridiculously well on that trip). I am very blessed to always have had a high level of fun. I know that when I die and people are talking about their memories of me, there will be many memories of fun times. Fun is the spice of life and, although being strong in Oola-Finance can provide you with endless opportunities, you can have free fun every day. I really encourage you to have fun every day of your life; you only get to live it once. No matter how you feel or how busy you are, take ten minutes and do something you enjoy. It will brighten the lives of those around you, provide you with a relaxing break, and help give purpose to the other six F's of Oola, all while bringing you closer to your OolaLife.

OOLAGURU

Fifty Countries and Counting

Without a doubt, my OolaFun is travel. I love seeing the United States, but my greater desire is to explore the world. I have traveled to fifty-plus countries and counting. I am built for adventure. I long for it, I look for it, I seek it out. International travel is a perfect fit for my love of life and desire to learn and grow.

When I travel, I don't just want to see the highlights, I want to immerse myself in the culture, eat what and where the locals eat, and do what they do. I'm more "backpack" than "cruise ship."

I travel against the grain. If I land in a foreign port and see a herd of tourists following a guide holding a flag on a stick, and they go left . . . I go right. If there is someone selling something from a make-shift grill on the back of a bike, I'm a buyer. I want to learn from the perspective and experiences of others. I believe everyone has something they can teach me to make me better. And I want to learn and be better.

One of my favorite places on the planet is Thailand, more specifically the island of Phuket. The culture and people are amazing. The demeanor of the Thai people is something to which I personally aspire. Some well-traveled people refer to Thailand as "LOS," for Land of Smiles. This is true. Everyone greets you with a smile, makes eye contact, and is very soft-spoken. It is an easy place to get off the well-traveled tourist track and meet some locals, and it won't take long to experience the grace of the Thai people.

The beaches are amazing. It is easy to avoid the busy ones (i.e., Patong Beach, Karon Beach, etc.) and rent a scooter and find a spot on the beaches less-traveled (i.e. Nai Thon Beach or Bang Tao Beach). You can treat yourself to an amazing massage on the

beach (a whopping $9 an hour) and find an expat to ask for a rec-
ommendation of a local Thai restaurant to cap off the day.

One of the reasons I like Phuket is that it's full of options. I love a
great beach as much as the next guy, but after a few hours I get
squirrely and need something to do. Renting scooters and explor-
ing the island is a nice way to spend a day. (Aside: You have to
be up for it. Traffic is crazy-awesome! It's like a video game.) You
can golf, take an elephant ride in the jungle, rent a long boat to a
remote island, or visit any of the countless restaurants (the seafood is
amazing).

There are other options for the easily bored, including many day
trips. If you get to Phuket you have to take a day boat trip to the Phi
Phi Islands. It is very touristy, but for a reason . . . it is probably one of
the most beautiful places on the planet (and where they filmed the
movie, *The Beach*). Find a little bar with a view (they all have views),
get something cold to drink, and soak in the beauty of what is in
front of you.

I have been to Thailand many times. However, it was my first trip
there with one of my best friends (the "horseshoe-up-the-ass" guy)
who made the biggest impression.

We went to Phuket purely on a vacation. We were working hard
in the region and needed a break. Many of the people we met
while working told us this is the must-go place in Asia. So with little
expectation or research, we spontaneously made the trip. It was
amazing. The people were awesome, the food incredible, the scenery beautiful. Our friends delivered on the recommendation; it was
as promised.

On December 26, 2004, just six weeks after returning from our
initial trip to Phuket, and with wonderful memories still fresh in our
minds and our tans barely faded, the historic tsunami devastated
the island. On the news, we saw images of destruction on the very

streets we had strolled, markets we had shopped, and the areas we had met new friends. Usually when seeing images on the news happening halfway around the world, the TV and the distance somehow make the tragedy feel less personal, less our problem. This recent trip made it real, painful, and personal.

We were not part of the recovery effort, but we did make a follow-up trip about a year later. Upon arrival, we felt we needed to do something. We didn't know what, but something. We identified an orphanage in a small village that was in need. We hired a driver with a truck and loaded the back with books, bikes, and toys and paid a visit. The kids' eyes lit up with joy. The director was grateful, very polite, and said all the right things. I can sniff out the difference between sincere gratitude and insincere gratitude a mile away. As I dug a little deeper, she told us she was grateful for our generosity, but that we had given what we felt the kids would need or want.

We didn't take the time to ask about the true needs of the kids. We were just another group of tourists dropping off some toys on their way to the beach. In retrospect, our hearts were in the right place, but our generosity misdirected. We needed to dig deeper into their true needs.

The director pointed out one boy in the group, Jinju. She asked me to guess his age. I have four kids of various ages, so I am pretty good at this game. I guessed three. He was eight. His growth was stunted from improper nutrition. She said what the kids really needed was some very basic nutrition.

Following that visit we came up with a program called "One Vitamin Per Child Per Day." Super simple, inexpensive, and on target. It's not enough . . . but a step in the right direction. (Aside: I am pleased to report that the program is still in place today and the orphanage has expanded its daycare facility to add a safe house and now helps various kids in need.)

My summary is this: My OolaFun is adventure and travel. Having fun is Oola. And that is enough. You need to have fun in life to be balanced. But if you can somehow link your fun to benefit others, the rewards will compound. That is Oola Plus One!

OOLAFUN TIPS:

1) **Discover**

We repeatedly ask people short on time and overwhelmed with family and work responsibilities, "What do you enjoy?" Sometimes they pause, tear up, and say, "I really don't know." Somehow, they have gotten so wrapped up in the day-to-day of the work and family responsibilities that they have lost touch with their personal passion. They have almost forgotten what they enjoy, on their own time. If this is you, discover (or rediscover) your OolaFun.

2) **Keep It in Check**

This is the opposite extreme of #1. This is when your activity or hobby takes over your life. This is when it is all you do all the time and it adversely affects the other F's of Oola. If you can't pay rent because you need a limited edition Star Wars figurine . . . you need to keep it in check. If you miss the soccer game because you are putting the final touches on the eighth scrapbook project for the week . . . you need to keep it in check. This book is about life balance. So balance your fun responsibly.

3) **Share**

To really grow your Oola in this category, we challenge you to merge what you love in a way that positively impacts others. If you love quilting, sell some, but also give some to a local raffle. If you are a golfer, join Big Brothers and take a kid golfing. There are countless ways to share what you love with others and make the world a better place, if only one interaction at a time. This experience will not distract from your fun, it will magnify it.

OOLABLOCKERS

*"Everybody has gone through something that
has changed them in a way that they could never
go back to the person they once were."*

— Leonardo DiCaprio

I f you truly have a desire to balance and grow your life, it is paramount that you identify those things that hold you back and those that propel you forward. We call these the OolaBlockers and the OolaAccelerators.

As you explore the next two sections, understand that there are countless traits and characteristics that drive us forward or get in our way. We picked seven of each, for the very simple reason that we like the number seven. Also, the seven we chose are the ones that personally have had the greatest impact on our journey to Oola. They are also the traits and characteristics that we commonly observe that affect the journeys of others.

In your case, you may be good-looking. That's an accelerator. We don't have that one. You may suffer from envy, that's an OolaBlocker. Thankfully, we don't have that one either. OolaBlockers and Oola-Accelerators are numerous. We are presenting the biggies, and we just want to be clear that the lists are not exclusive. We only share what we believe in our core and what we have seen work firsthand.

We're going to clean house first. Section Three deals with removing the OolaBlockers. This is the junk in your life that is holding you back from a life in Oola. Although it may be a challenge to look at yourself honestly, we know that by "cleaning your house" first, you can build from a fresh place. First, remove the crap that blocks your path. It is important to clear the way, so you don't step in the crap while you work toward the life you want. If you don't, you will step in it, it will stick on your shoes, it will slow you down, and it will smell.

In Section Four the fun begins. We introduce the OolaAccelerators and show you ways to get to Oola faster.

FEAR

"My motto is:
feel the fear and do it anyway."

—Tamara Mellon

F ear is first in our list of potential OolaBlockers by design. For most people, this is the greatest obstacle in their pursuit of Oola. Fear can get in the way of you getting the life you want in two ways: 1) unrealistic fear can paralyze you and prevent you from taking actions that will move you forward, and 2) a complete disregard of fear can expose you to risks that can take you down.

OOLASEEKER

Life Lessons from the Farm

I promise I won't continue to write about farm life in North Dakota, but my upbringing does come with its fair share of stories and learning experiences. My parents were hard workers . . . very hard! They rarely took time for themselves off the farm to enjoy an evening together. You know, go to the big city—a town of 800 people, half of whom are your relatives.

But I remember one particular evening they did. They were off on a date to the only cafe in town and we kids were home alone, just my sisters and me. We were watching one of the three TV channels available when we heard the sound of an intruder in the garage. We all looked at each other like it didn't really happen, but we all knew it did. Moments later we heard the intruder walk down the stairs to the basement door and begin knocking at the door, violently and repeatedly. My oldest sister did exactly what an older sister should do. She rounded us all up and took us to the bathroom, where we locked the door and huddled into the corner. She told us to remain calm and start praying the rosary. She told us that while we would most likely be murdered, at least we would go to heaven. Really?

After an hour or so of praying, our parents came home to the rescue. Who was the intruder? An overweight neighbor cat that had gotten into our garage, torn open the garbage, and got her head stuck in a Campbell's soup can. The cat then fell down the garage stairs and repeatedly ran into the basement door while trying to shake the can off her head. Fear? Absolutely! Justified? Hardly.

> **Unjustified fear paralyzes people. I see it all the time.**

I have used this story many times with friends and family over the years when they are experiencing the fear of a new job, a new relationship, or new direction for their life. I share with them the common acronym F.E.A.R., which stands for "False Expectations that Appear Real." The paralyzing effects of most fears are unjustified and hold us back from taking the necessary steps to a life more In Oola. Did I experience fear during my journey back to Oola? The answer is, "yes, and every day." Starting a new business, joining a gym, making new friends, and being a single father of five all can evoke fear. However, in the face of fear, I took action to focus on the big picture, stay true to my highest values, and overcome any fear blocking my path to the OolaLife.

OOLAGURU

The Safari Guide

When my oldest son was in fourth grade, we had the opportunity to go on an African safari. We were so excited that we counted the days. It was a first for both of us.

When the day finally arrived and we boarded the flight, we were filled with anticipation. The flight felt like forever.

It was night when we arrived at the Safari Camp. We were greeted by a very serious looking guy, wearing all the Safari Guy gear. He had the little tan hat with the rigid round brim, tightly-tied dark boots that went a third of the way up his shins, neatly-pressed pants with a ridiculous number of pockets, and a matching vest with enough widgets and tools to build a small house. Even with all his awesomeness, my son and I were most mesmerized by his big black gun. This wasn't your typical gun, it was special. We had never seen anything like it.

As I looked at this guide, I can remember thinking to myself, "Wow, this place does it right. They are really playing it up nice for my son. This really feels like an adventure. This is better than the Jungle Ride at Disney!"

After welcoming us, our guide informed us that we were in Villa #2, in the northeast corner of camp, just a short five-minute walk away. He said he would walk us to our villa. I replied, "No need. We will find our way." He then stated, "No, I must. It is not safe out here at night and I have a gun to protect you. In fact, do not leave your villa at night for any reason." I was even more impressed! This guy was really working it for a big tip. With my son not looking, I winked at him and said, "Seriously, I got this." His look changed from pleasant host to serious guide. He stared me straight in the eyes and said,

"Sir, I must walk you to your room. It is not safe here at night. We had an incident here once. It is camp policy." Needless to say, we graciously and gratefully accepted his offer and let him walk us to our villa.

Unjustified fear paralyzes people. I see it all the time. Someone is presented with a true opportunity. They analyze it to death thinking of every reason why it will not work. This fear keeps them from acting, and keeps them from growing. Fear blocks their path to Oola.

This story represents the other end of the spectrum relating to fear. If you completely disregard fear, you can get your head taken off, and in this example I mean that literally. It can be a game changer. I see this in business all the time. People go "all in" without calculating the risk. They lose their businesses, homes, families . . . their life. A complete disregard of fear will not block your way to Oola, it will quickly introduce you to the bottom.

Where are you relative to fear? Is fear preventing you from taking the action required to balance and grow your life? Are you stuck in a cycle of "analysis paralysis" where all you can focus on is what can go wrong if you chose to act? On the contrary, do you just run loose, completely void of fear in any situation? Search for the sweet spot in the middle. Free up this OolaBlocker in your life and you will be one step closer to the OolaLife.

GUILT

"Guilt: the gift that keeps on giving."

— Erma Bombeck

The weight of guilt is heavy. Guilt can build and become an OolaBlocker. We all make mistakes, and we all have said and done things that make us feel guilty. If the guilt is dealt with quickly, it will not do much to deviate you from your path to Oola. Persistent guilt, however, becomes a real OolaBlocker over time. It's that ongoing negative tug that many times accompanies guilt that can really hinder you from the life you want. It is like wearing five-pound ankle weights during a marathon. You may hardly know they are there during the first mile or two. But by mile twenty-two that extra subtle but persistent weight takes you down. If you have been on this planet more than three weeks, you have likely experienced guilt. Experiencing guilt is not the crime; choosing to carry guilt with you every day is.

OOLASEEKER ASIDE

The Drift

Of all the OolaBlockers in my life, none has been more prevalent than guilt. This was most obvious at my time visiting the bottom.

The slow downward spiral started seven years before my desperate phone call to the OolaGuru. I was at the top of my game and feeling invincible. My Oola was balanced and totally growing in all seven areas. On the periodic phone calls with the OolaGuru, I was proud to share my accomplishments and long list of successes. Even though I appeared humble on the outside, it was a false humility. I was so full of pride on the inside that it makes me sick to think about it today.

It was at this time that I let my first plate start to wobble. Could I really be this great? Is God giving me these gifts for a reason, or am I just above that and worthy of whatever I want? These thoughts alone, and the slow drift from OolaFaith, led me to the slippery slope that resulted in making choices completely inconsistent with my previous character. And oh, what a slippery slope it was!

> **Letting go of my guilt was my first step in climbing (no, scratching) my way up from the bottom of the barrel and getting my Oola back.**

These choices would eventually lead to me carrying heavy guilt for the next seven years. This guilt clouded my vision of the future, destroyed my self-worth, and made me question myself in all key areas of my life. Letting go of my guilt was my first step in climbing (no, scratching) my way up from the bottom of the barrel and getting my Oola back.

"Your past is in the rearview mirror, your future is spotless," said the OolaGuru. "Learn from the past, but don't continue to live in it. God forgave you even before you failed. Now all you need to do is to ask forgiveness from those you failed, and most important forgive yourself." To this day, that is the greatest lesson that I have learned from him.

OOLAGURU

The Skunk in the Window Well

We recently arrived at the cabin for the summer. When we get
there, I always do a quick walkthrough to see how the cabin handled the cold Minnesota winter. This year, I noticed a skunk in one of
the basement window wells. Unfortunately for him, he didn't survive
the winter. I only noticed a very faint odor coming from the skunk,
so I made sure the window was sealed and the shade closed. I then
went about enjoying my time with the family, the cabin, the lake . . .
the summer.

As the days and weeks passed I would occasionally get a whiff
of the skunk in the window well. It was enough to notice, enough
to wrinkle my nose, but it was subtle and eventually would pass. On
sunny days I would go into that bedroom, open the blind to allow
some light in, only to be reminded of my deceased friend, and
would quickly shut the blind again.

On a beautiful early summer day, I opened all the windows to
allow the fresh northern Minnesota air to flow through the cabin.
When I got to the basement bedroom, and opened the window, I
was blasted by a pungent odor. I was abruptly reminded of my problem. It could not be denied; today was the day I had the unpleasant
task of removing the skunk from the window well.

I will spare you the details and keep it short, but let me just say it
wasn't pretty—in sight or smell.

This is a true story, with a moral: It is important to confront the
unpleasant in your life quickly and directly. This applies to guilt, but
quite frankly any of the OolaBlockers in your life. If I had removed
the skunk on day one, it would have been easier to dispose of, and
caused less odor in my home and less guilt for my failure to confront

every time I saw or "scentced" him.

You can't just close the window and shut the blinds on the unpleasant in your life. The skunk will still be there. And if you can't see him, you will surely smell him from time to time. And the longer he sits there and festers and decomposes, the more difficult he will be to remove in the end.

No one is immune to guilt. We are human and we all make mistakes. Therefore, it is nearly impossible not to feel bad about our bad choices. We cannot avoid it. Guilt wears many faces and can hide deep in the recesses of your mind. Be mindful of where guilt resides in your life. Guilt is one of the sneakiest and most insidious of all the OolaBlockers. Sometimes it can hit you like a rock, other times it can present itself in more subtle ways.

Are you carrying the weight of guilt today? If so, rid yourself of carrying this burden. Regardless of the source of the guilt, it must be confronted. If you need help with this one, get it. Don't just shut the window and close the blinds. Otherwise, your guilt will fester and grow, holding you back from the life you deserve.

ANGER

"When angry, count to four;
when very angry, swear."

—Mark Twain

nger can come in many forms. It is normal to become upset or frustrated—these are common human emotions. However, being persistently or violently angry affects not just you, but everyone around you, and can bring consequences that you will live with forever. If you harbor anger and let it slowly eat away at your soul, it will destroy your chances for an OolaLife.

OOLASEEKER

Still Imprisoned

People who know me will say that I always seem happy, and I truly am. Even on my worst days, I inherently carry an upbeat attitude toward life. I have seen anger as a major OolaBlocker for friends and family over the years, but I can honestly and thankfully say that this is a low-risk block for me. I have seen my father and his brothers discuss politics and get angry to the point of ruining an otherwise enjoyable Sunday afternoon. Husbands get angry with wives, brothers get angry with sisters, and parents get angry with children. The biggest block formed from anger is actually the harboring of anger for years after the wrongdoing has taken place.

I heard a story a while back that describes the effects of holding on to anger this way. It starts with a clean-cut, well-dressed man in his midfifties walking along the Vietnam Memorial with his wife and family. He was a former POW and had made the journey to Washington, D.C., to pay his respects to the fallen soldiers. During this walk, he coincidentally ran into his cellmate from when he was imprisoned. This man had quite the opposite look. Dirty clothes, long straggly hair, unshaven, and unbathed would describe him best. The homeless-looking man started in immediately, "I hate what they did to us in that prison camp. I think of it every day and I am so angry. The torture, the starvation, and the sleeping conditions . . . I will never forgive them and I will always hate them. It is because of them that I have addictions. It is because of them that I cannot get a job and became homeless. It is because of them that I lost my family." The well-dressed man stopped him mid-sentence and said, "Why do you

> **"Anger can be a bump in the road or it can be a block."**

still allow them to keep you locked up in their prison? You were freed more than thirty years ago."

Anger can be a bump in the road or it can be a block. Be careful not to let the consequences of your harbored anger turn into a concrete wall preventing you from an OolaLife.

OOLAGURU

The Cracked Windshield

Anger is a powerful emotion. It takes many forms and degrees. Thankfully, anger does not block me. Frustration, however, I can relate to. I sometimes let the small things get to me. My reaction is stronger than it needs to be. My response is not always proportional to the situation.

Today was a perfect example. While sitting with the OolaSeeker at the lake trying to rip out this book, we heard the faint sound of our kids' voices from across the water. We left our keyboards and checked it out. We looked across the lake and saw two groups of kids waving their hands trying to get our attention. Both groups were ours. One group was in the fishing boat and the other on a Sea-Doo . . . both out of gas. This is a very small issue in the grand scheme of life. I get that but, nonetheless, I was frustrated. Repeated reminders to check for gas before they went out for the day apparently fell on deaf ears.

Thankfully, my frustration was brief. It was remedied by something I learned from the OolaSeeker. It was on my last trip to the mountains to visit him in one of our coaching sessions. He was off the bottom and getting his Oola back. He had recently purchased a "new to him" car. It was a late model Land Rover, a long way from the crappy Taurus. It was a nice car. We were driving down the highway and we heard an incredibly loud noise. A stone rolled off the bed of a landscape truck in front of us, immediately cracking the windshield from end to end. Not only was I startled, I felt for him. If not angry, I would understand if he were frustrated in the moment. However, immediately after we realized what had happened, he simply turned up the music, looked at me, smiled, and said, "Hakuna Matata, no

worries, it is in the past. Nothing we can do about it now." He continued driving down the highway as if nothing happened.

I still reflect upon this lesson when I feel frustration. Ongoing anger
can lead to nasty things, like not forgiving, resentment, and perpetual negativity. So whenever I feel frustrated or angry, I remind
myself that it is blocking me from my life in Oola and picture the
OolaSeeker smiling and looking though the damaged windshield as
if the crack wasn't even there.

If you feel angry or are easily frustrated, listen to what the world
is telling you. What did you learn from the wrongdoing? How may
this wrongdoing have shifted you in a different direction? Could the
guy that just cut you off in traffic keep you from a car accident ten
minutes down the road? Did your abusive father help make you more
independent? Was the cheating spouse and eventual divorce a start
to a new life? This is a great emotion to evaluate and learn from in
your life, but don't allow this emotion to get in the way of your life
. . . your OolaLife.

CHAPTER

13

SELF-SABOTAGE

"You're imperfect, and you're wired for struggle,
but you are worthy of love and belonging."

— Brené Brown

Y ou may notice a recurring theme in this book, especially in the OolaBlocker section. No matter what you have done or failed to do up to this point, you are deserving of an OolaLife. Simply, you are designed by God for greatness and a purpose, so please do not work hard at balancing and growing your life only to get right to the verge of Oola and blow it through self-sabotage.

When examining all the OolaBlockers, this is the most subconscious block of them all. It is an all-too-common cycle. You worked hard to identify exactly where you are in the 7 F's of Oola, you developed an OolaPlan and followed the OolaPath. Your growth took effort and sacrifice. You begin to reap tangible rewards of your effort and sacrifice. Your stress begins to ease, you feel more balanced, you are inspired by your growth. You feel the momentum gained by the pursuit of a balanced life. You feel on track to discover your personal destiny. Then one day, all the subconscious negative self-talk speaks up, and you decide that you are not worth it and you unknowingly begin the process of self-sabotage. STOP. Once again, no matter what, NO MATTER WHAT, hear us when we say that you deserve all your wildest dreams to come true. Your Oola awaits.

OOLASEEKER

The White Picket Fence Life

When I think of all the OolaBlockers, the one that repeatedly gets the most "credit" for my fall from Oola is guilt. But, is that fair to guilt? Maybe there was a precursor, a hidden contributor buried deep in my subconscious. Why did I even let that first plate start to wobble in the first place? Of course I was living in ego. Of course I was cocky. But I still question if there was an additional contributing factor. Unfortunately, I have to say yes to these questions . . . all of them.

The OolaGuru and I were very close a long time ago. We were great friends with similar thoughts, dreams, and aspirations. We kept in touch constantly. We shared our dreams, compared goals, wrote plans, and aspired to balance and grow. Why did the two roads diverge? Was it because I did what I thought I was supposed to do and the Guru did what his heart told him to do?

One of our biggest dreams was to start an international business somewhere cool in the world. When this opportunity materialized for the Guru, he followed his destiny. He had no hesitation in leaving a great job. He picked up his wife and three small kids and moved halfway around the world to pursue an amazing business opportunity.

No matter what, NO MATTER WHAT, hear us when we say that you deserve all your wildest dreams to come true.

With my head leading the way, I chose the safe white picket fence life—the steady income, the predictable friends, boating on the river, and the typical American dream. But, every day my heart felt like I was not in the right place. I did not listen to the unspoken nudge to follow my true purpose. Which to this day

still raises the question, "Did I ignore that initial wobbly plate on purpose?" Did I somehow sabotage my own life just to get out of one
situation I did not want to be in, to open up the opportunity to where
my heart wanted to go? Because self-sabotage is such a silent killer
of Oola, I think it's a possibility. I think it snuck up on me slowly and
without warning and bit me in the ass . . . hard. Guilt, self-sabotage
. . . it is hard to tell where it started and how to apportion blame to
the greatest contributor to my demise. The one thing I know for
certain is that both are, without a doubt, serious OolaBlockers.

OOLAGURU

A Lesson from a Guru's Guru

Paulo Coelho, in the introduction to his international bestselling book, *The Alchemist*, paints a clear written picture of the obstacles preventing us from our personal calling. Regarding the fourth and final obstacle he states, "Oscar Wilde said: 'Each man kills the thing he loves.' And it's true. The mere possibility of getting what we want fills the soul of the ordinary person with guilt. We look around at all those who have failed to get what they want and feel that we do not deserve to get what we want either. We forget about all the obstacles we overcame, all the suffering we endured, all the things we had to give up in order to get this far. I have known a lot of people who, when their personal calling was within their grasp, went on to commit a series of stupid mistakes and never reached their goal—when it was only a step away."

Self-sabotage intrigues me. I have studied the phenomenon and still can't grasp it intellectually. Like gravity, I don't have to under-stand it to know it exists. I know it exists because I have seen it in action, many times over. I have great respect for its power to destroy dreams.

The OolaSeeker's transparent story is a clear example of how his missed opportunity contributed to his fall. How many times have you seen a friend or loved one sacrifice to lose a bunch of weight only to gain it back when they were within reach of their goal? I repeatedly see people work hard for years to reach their goal, only to insert a heavy dose of procrastination and indecisiveness or poor choices at the last minute, resulting in failure with the finish line in sight.

Learn what I learned from one of my gurus, Paulo Coelho: ". . . if you believe yourself worthy of the thing you fought so hard to get, then you become an instrument of God, you help the Soul of the World, and you understand why you are here."

If you can grasp and own this concept, you will be able to avoid this powerful OolaBlocker.

◎ ◎ ◎ ◎

This book is going to provide you with a simple three-step guide to balance and grow your life. We will also clearly outline the seven key areas that lead to an awesome life. The three steps are simple; the seven key areas are clear. Please do not go through the effort of reading this book, learning the 7 F's of Oola, completing an OolaWheel, following the OolaPlan, and following the OolaPath only to sabotage all the gains realized in a public display of subconscious self-destruction. Know you are worthy and designed by God for greatness and a purpose. Keep your mind and arms open to change, embrace balance and growth, and go get the life you deserve. Don't just see the finish line, cross the finish line.

LAZINESS

"*You must avoid sloth, that wicked siren.*"

— Horace

Think of your favorite athlete of all time. Who is your favorite actor, actress, or performer? Think of the most influential business and world leaders. Anyone at the top of their game has one thing in common—they are not lazy. They are passionate about their life and worked very hard to get to the top. On the path to Oola there is no room for lazy. It cannot be part of your life in any way, shape, or form. In short, lazy blocks Oola.

Some of you may be fairly balanced and growing the life of your dreams, maybe even living the OolaLife. If so, it will take effort to maintain and continue to grow, but not the intense effort of someone who is way out of Oola. For those of you living it, we have faith that you will put forth the effort to continue in your sweet state. For those of you on the bottom, or climbing your way up, we promise you it is worth all the blood, sweat, and tears it may take to get to your OolaLife.

OOLASEEKER

All In

Here is a general picture of many of my days as a single dad scraping my way back to Oola during the past three years of my life:

2:00 a.m.: Go to bed.

6:40 a.m.: My annoying iPhone starts its happy-ass wake-up ringtone. I wake up the kids for school and get my shower on.

7:40 a.m.: The kids are all dropped off and I head through Java Joes, my favorite coffee shop. And, yes, they know me on a first-name basis!

8:00 a.m.: My day job begins.

7:00 p.m.: My day job ends. Pick up kids, finish soccer carpool, head home to start the homework chain and let the evening wind down.

10:00 p.m.: Kids are asleep and I start my second job— The Oola start-up.

REPEAT

Are you thinking, *Man, this guy is out of Oola. This doesn't sound like a balanced and growing life to me!* If you are thinking that, you're wrong! It is balanced and growing. But, over the last three years it had to balance and grow from the bottom up. And yes, that took serious effort. There was no room for laziness, none whatsoever!

The OolaLife will take effort, but the rewards are deep and the fruits produced, sweet.

Now that I am closer to my OolaLife I have a hard time even comprehending the effort, the pain, and the hard work that went into getting my Oola back. But if I had to,

I would do it all again. The deep state of fulfillment associated with a life in Oola is just too great not to work for it.

Now that my Oola is coming back, I sold my former businesses and work on my Oola companies full time. I rarely miss a soccer game, I took the kids on a ten-day trip through France, I'm on track to be debt free by year end, I work out five days a week, and I feel lean and mean. Most important, my family is doing amazingly well. Was it worth the work and the effort? Was it worth not being lazy? I won't even answer. Results speak.

OOLAGURU

Now Hiring

Everything is designed to make things easier. Stated another way, everything is designed so that we can expend less effort. If we are not careful, this can lend us to a life of laziness. A life of laziness will prevent you from an OolaLife.

Thankfully, today we don't have to get out of a car and manually open the garage door, we push a button. We don't have to get off the couch to change the channel, we push a different button. We don't have to push a lawn mower, we sit on it. We don't have to spend three hours in the kitchen preparing a meal, we can call someone to bring it right to our door.

I love efficiency. I respect efficiency. I am grateful for advancement and technology that makes life more efficient. However, we need to be careful to not let our cultural love of efficiency lead to laziness in areas of our lives that require effort.

If you are a dude and your boobs jiggle as you roll down the highway, don't buy a magic pill. Find a gym. If you are in debt, don't reflexively file for bankruptcy. Dig in, get a second job, control your spending, see if there is a way out. If your marriage wobbles, don't call for the "$99 divorce today." Work at it, see if there is something to reconcile. If you lack purpose in life, do not sit and let life pass you by. Seek knowledge to find your place in this world. If you lose your job, pick up an employment application *before* an unemployment application.

My family and I were driving through town recently. We stopped at the light. On the opposite side of the road, sitting on the curb, was a man. He looked rough. Unshaven, clothes tattered, shoulders slumped, head down, holding a bucket and a sign. The sign read,

"Need Work. God Bless." My family, in unison, rallied for me to fill his bucket. I told them to look over his left shoulder, in the distance, just across the highway. There they could see the familiar golden arches. The marquee read simply, "Now Hiring." I don't claim to know this man's individual circumstances, but I remember thinking, "This man does not need to pick up a sign, he needs to pick up a pen, cross the road, and fill out an application."

This may come across as a little harsh. I am not saying that bad things can't happen to good people and you shouldn't rely on the help of others or programs that are out there (there are many great charities out there—we love, Asia Center Foundation, Rice Bowls, and First Things First Foundation, just to name a few). But when taking assistance, make sure that the help empowers you, not enables you. There is self-worth and momentum in making the effort to do the right thing that cannot be measured.

The OolaLife is simple to attain, but it is not easy. There is no room for laziness on the path to Oola. This will take effort, but the rewards are deep and the fruits produced, sweet. As you take steps toward Oola, you just watch—your shoulders will go back, your chest out, head up, and you will get off the curb.

ENVY

"Envy is the art of counting the other fellow's blessings instead of your own."

—Harold Coffin

Envy and jealousy are related. They are in the same family. They will both block your path to Oola. Envy is the worse of two evils. The difference between envy and jealousy is this: You are jealous if you want what others have. You suffer from envy if you not only want what others have, but you also want to make sure they don't have it. Both are nasty and can suck the joy out of life.

OOLASEEKER

The Black Ninja

The summer of 1986 was the first and last time that I felt envious or jealous in my life. I don't feel like envy is an OolaBlocker for me, but I know that it exists and can keep people from their well-deserved OolaLife because I had a brush with it.

If you grew up in the '80s like I did, you most likely wanted to marry Tom Cruise (for the ladies), or be like him (for the guys). The scene from Top Gun when Maverick is flying down the road on his black Ninja crotch rocket will be burned into my brain forever. I wanted that bike. I wanted to fly down the road on a black Ninja so badly. I was somewhat obsessed.

The scene from *Top Gun* when Maverick is flying down the road on his black Ninja crotch rocket will be burned into my brain forever.

Remember, my experience on a bike up to this point was my hand-me-down pink Huffy three-speed. But, how hard could that Ninja be to drive? I was sure I could learn. If I could get past the financial obstacle of having only $100 to my name, I was in. The girls would dig me and I would be the man. Plan set in motion: Start saving money and practice riding the pink Huffy three-speed faster and with more testosterone. A month into grinding out this plan, the most devastating thing happened to me, and his name was James.

When you grow up in a small town, there is a serious shortage of available young ladies, and the competition for them is fierce. You have seen the documentary with the two rams fighting to the death on a mountainside—it's that kind of serious. So when James drove up to the party on his new black Ninja, it was on! I was wishing that he would wreck it. Thoughts of the bike skidding down the street with sparks flying crossed my mind. Look at him: He thinks he is totally cool right now! Jealousy and envy were understatements for my feelings at that moment.

It was a Thursday. James let one of my good friends (who had experience with motorcycles) drive the Ninja for the evening. This was my chance. I convinced my buddy Chris to let me ride it. It was amazing. I looked awesome as I slowly cruised through town. I envisioned myself looking exactly like Tom Cruise.

I was the man for exactly four minutes. Because that's how long it took me to learn that the Ninja was way more powerful than the pink Huffy. I crashed the bike and I was the guy road-rashing down the street before landing next to the dumped and scratched-to-crap Ninja. Humiliation at its finest. Chalk another one up to lessons learned . . . the hard way!

I spent the rest of the summer working just to pay back my dad for the repairs. To this day, my dad still thinks that I backed into the Ninja with my car. I am looking forward to the phone call when my dad gets to this chapter. This event proved that envy is not for me. To this day I do not have envy as an OolaBlocker. And I have never been back on a Ninja or street bike of any kind!

OOLAGURU

My Brother and the Flaming Pinto

I have an amazing older brother. He is eight years older than me. To this day, he is one of my gurus, my friend, my 24/7 mentor. Growing up, he looked after me and my well-being. He is still that way today.

We had the classic suburban middle class big brother/little brother relationship. Our family consisted of four kids and three small bedrooms. You do the math. My brother was stuck with me, in the same bed, every night. I was blessed with a loving father who worked hard to provide for a family of six. Very hard. He worked two jobs and weekends to provide. Without being asked, my brother took on some extra responsibilities. He taught me to golf, to appreciate good music (I wore out his Peter Frampton eight-track), to love cars, and to respect people. He gave me a solid moral foundation.

I was ten when my brother moved out of the house. Although the house felt empty and my heart felt a bit the same way, my brother left to become a man in the world. His successes were swift and many. He found a great wife, locked into the fast track in an amazing career, and quickly began to acquire the material successes that smart work and discipline provide. He had a new Corvette at nineteen, a summer place on the lake by twenty-seven, and soon thereafter a place on the beach in California—all while raising a beautiful family of five.

To set the stage, at the time the OolaLife was rolling for my brother, I was gutting it out in college. I drove a mud-brown Pinto with a puke-orange vinyl interior (which eventually caught fire and was left on the side of the road for the fire department to deal with). I was deep into student loan debt and crossing my fingers that I would somehow get a good enough job to pay them back some-day. I was single. I was faithless. My only friends were those in my class. I weighed nearly 200 pounds (I am now 160). You would think I would be jealous or envious of my big brother. I wasn't, not once, not a bit, not ever.

It must be that golden horseshoe up my butt. Envy is not in me, and I attribute the lack of envy as a contributor to my OolaLife. I think this stems from my belief in infinite opportunities. To explore this further, it is worth looking at two opposing philosophies regarding resources. For this example let's use money.

Let's say Bob has a million dollars. Does that mean there is a million less dollars available for the rest of the world? This is what I refer to as a FINITE look at opportunities. People with this outlook on life have a tendency toward jealousy and envy. They believe that if you've got it they can't have it, like you took theirs. I believe this is wrong.

I look at opportunities as INFINITE. Consider the example of a room full of unlit candles. Picture a dark gymnasium. In it there are two-foot by two-foot school desks evenly placed one foot apart. The school desks fill the entire gym floor. Centered on each desk is an unlit candle. Lights are off in the gym, and the room is dark. I walk into the gym with my candle fully lit. I enter the room and light the first candle on the first desk. I then take that candle and light the candle next to it, and the one next to it, and so on. In a relatively short period of time, every candle on every desk is lit. The room is filled with glowing light from the collective candles, and my candle remains unchanged, lit and shining brightly.

This example demonstrates that if someone else has an OolaLife, it is still available to you. Opportunities are limitless. Provide some-thing of value, something of service, to the world and you will be rewarded. Light the candles of others and light up the room. If you see the world in this way it is impossible to feel envy or jealousy and your path to the OolaLife will be clear.

Zig Ziglar once said,"In order to get what you want, help others get what they want." Envy and jealousy are evil. These feelings do not bring you what others have, they bring you further away. Nothing good resides in them. Avoid them. If others have what you want, don't become jealous, become inspired. They represent what is possible. You are worthy and have the talents and abilities to get what you want out of life. Serve the world and it will serve you. Help people and they will help you. Remember that opportunities are INFINITE, not FINITE. Reject envy and jealousy and go light up the world!

FOCUS

"I fear not the man who has practiced
10,000 kicks once, but I fear the man who has
practiced one kick 10,000 times."

—Bruce Lee

F
ocus is clearly an OolaAccelerator. It can, however, morph into an OolaBlocker if it takes one of two forms: 1) lack of focus, or 2) misdirected focus.

Lack of focus is the most common of the two. If you lack focus, you cannot endure what it takes to balance and grow. The journey to Oola is not for the weak. You have to focus not just on the moment, but in the distance, on the larger goal: a life balanced and growing in all 7 F's of Oola . . . the OolaLife.

In a culture of buy now, pay later, the supersized meal (with a Diet Coke), I want what I want and I want it now . . . it is becoming counterculture to delay gratification for a larger goal. Delayed gratification is Oola. Focusing on the larger goal will give you the strength you need to sacrifice now in order to win later.

Lack of focus does just the opposite. If you lack focus on your distant but more noble goals, you will buy what you want when you want, eat what you want when you want, be in a relationship only until it hits its first bump, sit in front of the TV instead of play with the kids, and choose to sleep in on Sunday instead of checking out a place of faith. You will live only in the now and wake up years later and wonder why all the plans and dreams when you were younger never materialized. We are all for seizing the day, but with an asterisk. A more Oola motto is, "Live like you're going to die tomorrow, but plan like you're going to live forever."

Misdirected focus is less common than lack of focus, but can be equally counter-productive in your pursuit of Oola. Misdirected focus is focus directed at anything

> **Had it, lost it, getting it back, and NEVER losing it again!**

NOT in the 7 F's of Oola. Addictions are the obvious example of misdirected focus. Drugs, alcohol, pornography, gambling, and other addictions don't just block the path to the OolaLife, they can suck all the Oola out of one's life. Think about the classic addict in relation to the 7 F's of Oola: fitness (none), financial (broke), family (divorced and alone), field (unemployed), faith (serving only the addiction), friends (none, other than fellow addicts and codependents), and fun (none). That is the definition of anti-Oola and just with this Oola-Blocker, misdirected focus.

OOLASEEKER

Never Again

HAD IT, LOST IT, GETTING IT BACK!

Up to this point in the book, you have seen this slogan become a popular theme when reading my stories. If you follow me on Twitter, Facebook, or the OolaBlog you will see the same. I repeat these seven words many times a day in my head, but my version has a slight twist. It goes more like this, "Had it, lost it, getting it back, and NEVER losing it again!" Everyone who has had a taste of an OolaLife and lost it understands exactly what I mean. Losing what you have worked so hard for is painful. The scar left from this pain reminds me to never again lose focus on my pursuit of the OolaLife.

When I first met the OolaGuru more than fifteen years ago, we would regularly devote three straight days to working on Oola. The whole point of the retreat was to balance and grow. Day one would be focused on where we were at that time. Day two was dedicated to planning where we wanted to go in our lives. And the third day was devoted to designing a path that would lead us to our OolaLife. I always looked forward to these meetings. We met in really cool places and tapped into each other's knowledge, creativity, and support to build a great plan and design an achievable path. I was like a kid heading to Disney World. I would be excited the entire week before. The week after I would be exhausted but refocused and recharged for the growth that lay ahead. Focusing on the objective, on the OolaLife, was a key factor in being successful in following my path.

Focus was never a block for me when I was in pursuit of Oola or when I was living the OolaLife. I had so much drive and so much passion toward my goals that my only issue was not being able to turn my focus off when I went to bed.

However, when I was at the bottom, it was challenging to find the focus required to dig my way out of the mess. Intellectually, I knew I needed to find balance and grow, but it was rough. One phone call from a creditor, one look in the mirror, or the sight of one duffle bag packed for five kids to stay at dad's place, were constant reminders of my current state of un-Oola and would suck the focus right out of me. Thankfully, I would dig deep and always seem to find my focus. Whether you have it, had it, or are trying to get it back, remain focused on the outcome and importance of a balanced and growing life. And if you're lucky enough to get it, stay focused and never lose it.

OOLAGURU

_____

Lost in the Arabian Gulf

I was in Abu Dhabi on business. We were out to dinner with a group of friends. The conversation was nice, bouncing around from topic to topic. When the topic landed on fitness, we stuck there for a while. Everyone wished they were more fit. We were at that age. We were all trying to squeeze it in, but nothing was too consistent.

One of my friends mentioned that there was a triathlon at Al Raha Beach the next morning. His buddy was organizing the event and we could easily get in. My personality has always been "ready, fire, aim," so I was the first to pop up. I ended up being the only one at the table to commit.

I was an okay runner, but my only swimsuit was a pair of board shorts and I didn't even have a bike. One of the guys at the table quickly volunteered his bike, so I guess that excuse didn't fly. No backing out now.

The next morning I woke early so I could swing by and pick up the loaner bike on the way to the race. When I got there, I couldn't believe what I saw. He had a bike all right, but it was an old, over-sized (he's six-foot-three) mountain bike. Wrapped around the seat stem was a lock that looked like an Alaskan logging chain. A racing bike it was not. I asked if he could at least remove the heavy chain to lighten it up a bit; he replied, "Sorry, I forgot the combo." To this day I am 100 percent certain that the chain alone weighed more than the average bike in the race.

No worries. I show up to the starting line in my board shorts and log-chain bike. When I get there I immediately notice a group of guys on the floor shaving their legs. I knew I was in trouble. My fears were confirmed when, just prior to the race, I hear over the loud speaker, "Introducing, the number two in the world, from Sweden, Sven So-n-So." The introductions for the top triathletes in the world continued for what felt like an eternity. It was the inaugural event, and when they do it in the Emirates, they do it big. They flew in the best. And I'm right there with them in my board shorts and with my loaner log-chain bike.

The gun sounded, the swim began. It was all a blur. It was in the ocean, and at that time my only experience swimming was to the side of the pool to get a cold drink. It took all the focus I had just to keep my head above water and limbs moving. The swim felt like an eternity. I kept my head up, and my stroke churning. This was a sprint triathlon, so I kept thinking that this shouldn't be taking this long.

When I finally looked up to check on my progress, there were no swimmers in sight. I couldn't even see the finish line. My focus had been on keeping my head up and arms and legs moving, but not on the target. My focus was misdirected and my friends were on the beach, pointing, laughing, and watching the entire time.

Focus is usually associated as a trait that can propel you toward Oola. However, if in the form of "lack of focus" or "misdirected focus," it is a clear OolaBlocker. Zig Ziglar has a classic quote, "If you aim at nothing you will hit it every time." Focus on the dream life you desire, don't get misdirected, and the OolaLife is yours.

OOLAACCELERATORS

"Greatness is not this wonderful, esoteric, elusive,
god-like feature that only the special among us will ever
taste, it's something that truly exists in all of us."

— Will Smith

The last section dealt with OolaBlockers. OolaBlockers are evil. Rid your life of any and all OolaBlockers. They are toxic on many levels and will get in the way of the life you desire and deserve.

This section deals with OolaAccelerators. OolaAccelerators are awesome. They are the traits and characteristics that will propel you to the OolaLife faster. If OolaBlockers are everything evil, Oola-Accelerators are everything good. Study them, focus on them, practice them, and invite them into your life.

OolaAccelerators will simply get you to Oola faster. Period.

GRATITUDE

"In all things, be grateful and have faith."

—@OolaSeeker

f you want to fast-track your journey to Oola, inject some gratitude. Be grateful for and love where you are, where you want to go,
and where you have been. Be grateful for *every* part of the journey.
Love is the key that unlocks the abundance that you deserve. Gratitude is the doorway from which it comes. The more grateful you are,
the more open you are to receive.

Gratitude can be very easy, but it can also be very complex to
understand. It is very easy to be grateful for all the good stuff. You
can be grateful for your family, your home, your car, and your job.
You can be grateful for green lights, sunny days, a light breeze, or the
perfect wave. But, can you be grateful for the red lights, the rainy days,
a crazy wind, or no waves at all? We believe you can.

Of course, we all know many people who would complain that
the green light was too green, the sunny day was too sunny, the wind
too windy, and "who cares about waves" since they don't surf or like
the sound of the ocean anyway. We might have even had some days
like these ourselves. If you have, how did you feel? Open to receive
or closed for business?

Now, let's take it a little deeper and consider the really bad stuff. Is
it possible to be grateful for losing your job, getting in an accident, or
having a sick child? These can get very difficult. The hidden gifts from
these so-called bad things can take months, years, or a lifetime to be
revealed. Understanding human emotion will tell you that it is okay
to be sad, angry, frustrated, or downright mad over certain situations,
but the faster you see the purpose and become truly grateful for the
experience, the more the door opens.

OOLASEEKER

JJ Strong

While writing this book, the Guru and I had many watery-eye moments. Most of the times our eyes were tearing up from laughing so hard at our experiences and the stories, sometimes painful, of our lives. But other times our eyes filled up with tears because of sheer gratitude. We share a common perspective. We are grateful for all the blessings that have been granted upon us, good and bad. Watery eyes happen when you are in the deepest form of gratitude, and it is a very special place. I want every one of you to experience such great levels of gratitude that you get a tear in your eye.

As I mentioned earlier, I have four sisters, all of whom I get along with great and love dearly. I have a very unique relationship with the sister closest in age to me—she is three years older. I have certainly spent the most time with her. We did farm chores together and rode in the car to football and basketball practices. Like a normal sister and brother relationship, we had our fights, but most of the time we got along great. When I picture gratitude, all I can think about is her and her story, which not only changed my life but also changed the lives of hundreds of thousands (literally).

My sister was peacefully living the life of her dreams. She lived the OolaLife. She married her high school sweetheart, Yendor. She was raising four beautiful, intelligent, and athletic kids and enjoyed painting on the side . . . very Oola! She loved her life and she was great at it.

During my slide to the bottom she was my rock. I called her on a daily and sometimes hourly basis. She was a great support for me. She always took my calls and calmed me down if I was stressed. "Everything happens for a reason," she always told me, "so be grateful and everything will be okay."

Later that year, the high school football season rolled around. Her second oldest son, Jared, a junior, was a 6-foot-2, 195-pound starting running back. To say that he was fast and athletic would be an understatement. Not only fast and athletic, but smart (as in "ass"), good-looking, hardworking, and one of the funniest guys I have ever known. This was going to be Jared's year. He got respectable playing time his sophomore season and now he had two years to lock in his college football scholarship.

During the preseason, Jared started getting nagging hip and low back pain. Since Jared isn't the kind of kid that complains, they took him to the doctor. After shooting some X-rays, the doctor noticed a concerning spot on his pelvic bone. Follow-up tests were needed. It didn't look good.

Roles quickly reversed. My issues seemed small and it was now my job to say, "Everything happens for a reason, be grateful and everything will be okay." I remember feeling so bad that my sister had to be stressed and worried while waiting for test results. I questioned the "everything happens for a reason" thing and, although I believed wholeheartedly in "count your blessings," it was hard to be grateful at moments like this. It was these circumstances, in fact, that created the tipping point that lead me to The Call to the Guru.

A short time later, the doctor confirmed that it wasn't just back strain, but a very serious form of bone cancer. At that moment, the world stopped for my sister and her husband and they had to start making choices that no parent should have to make. The doctor gave Jared less than a 10 percent chance of survival and informed them that the treatment would be very harsh. Jared quickly stated that a 10 percent

We challenge you to search for gratitude, not only in the good, but in the so-called bad moments in your life.

chance is pretty good, since he was normally in the top 10 percent of everything that he did. He informed the doctors and his family that everything happens for a reason, everything will be fine, and to bring it on. I think it is easier for a sixteen-year-old to feel invincible, but not so easy for his parents.

My sister, her amazing husband, and their family became dedicated to getting Jared well. The chemo and radiation treatments began. When he could, Jared miraculously continued to play football during his treatments. He ran like crazy, scored touchdowns, and always maintained a positive attitude. My sister and I talked often, and the majority of our conversations started or ended with what she was stressed about and what she was grateful for. Gratitude was our word. We spoke of it often and used it as a tool to get through all the craziness that comes with cancer.

Jared made it through the radiation and chemo treatments and his surgery to remove the tumor was successful. Jared went to prom, and in the spring he graduated from high school. He influenced so many people and often stated that he knew the reason that he had cancer. It was his destiny to teach everyone about being strong. His strength, in fact, started a "JJ Strong" movement. Everyone was wearing JJ Strong T-shirts and wristbands. Jared's CaringBridge site had over 200,000 visits from people following his progress.

The summer after Jared graduated, he was diagnosed with a rare form of leukemia that is brought on by harsh chemotherapy and radiation treatments. Another full-on fight began. My sister and I continued talking on a daily basis, more about her current situation than mine. After months of fighting, Jared's body had had enough. With his mother and father by his side, he took his last breath and left our family. Before he died, he told my sister that he was grateful that he got cancer instead of his sister or brothers, his friends, or the rest of the members of our family. He was grateful that God chose him for this.

Everything happens for a reason: Jared has inspired people to tuck their kids in a little longer at night. He has inspired people to pray harder and love deeper. If I live to be ninety years old, it will be hard to live up to the legacy left by my nephew. I have dedicated my life to making every day count, making the world a better place, and helping others around the world live happier and better lives, the OolaLife. I am dedicated to this in honor of Jared. I wear the JJ Strong wristband every day and will wear one the rest of my life (I have a bag of 100) as a reminder to always "Stay Strong— JJ Strong" for my purpose in life.

Be Grateful: I remain so grateful for everything in my life. Everything good reaffirms my purpose and every challenge redirects my actions. I am grateful for all of it. I really don't know how my sister and her husband make it through every day since Jared's death, but I am grateful for their strength and their faith as an example for myself and many others.

Everything will be okay: We are born, we live, and then we die. All of us follow the same path. Some are here for seconds and some are here for 100-plus years. We are all here for a reason and a purpose. Go with your heart, aspire to balance and grow, live your purpose, no, FIGHT for your purpose, and I do believe . . . everything will be okay!

OOLAGURU

Gift in Guangzhou

I have kept a daily journal since buying my first computer in 1988. I use a personal journal to keep track of events, travel, thoughts, and feelings. I share it with no one. It is just for me. My own way to record, reflect, even vent. I end each entry with "G" followed by a space. The "G" stands for gratitude. In the space I write at least one thing I am grateful for every day. You see, gratitude has a way of pushing all the negativity out of my body. I have found that when I feel deeply grateful, my body fills with happy molecules, leaving no room for the toxic ones.

All of us have those special thoughts or memories that trigger gratitude. The "goosebump, hair-raising, tear-in-the-eye" memories. For me it's my four kids. I can be tough in almost any situation, but put me in front of one of my kids performing, receiving an award, celebrating a special birthday, graduating from anything, leaving for college, even just sitting around the dinner table, and I have the ability to turn into a puddle at any moment. I don't know what it is, but whatever it is, it is not getting better as I get older. It is borderline embarrassing. I have seen this behavior in my own father, so maybe it's hereditary. I tolerate this behavior only because I know my tears are based in gratitude.

We have three biological children and we adopted our youngest daughter from China. The adoption of our daughter was a very emotional time. We knew Alea was a part of our family even before she was born. Our family was awesome, but there was a small hole that we knew she would fill perfectly.

The adoption process is long. Longer than it needs to be. Anyone who has been though the process will back me on this. It felt like forever to find out if and when we would be approved for an international adoption. After months and what felt like a thorough interrogation (fingerprints and all), we were finally approved. The next step was to wait. We were told we would receive our match in the mail. We felt Alea in our hearts for years, but now we would finally get to see a photo. We would be able to match the image in our mind to the image in a photo. We could hardly wait. Each hour felt like a day, every day felt like a week. The mail would come, and the mail would go. Still no photo.

One sunny July day, with tears in her eyes, my wife walked into the house carrying a manila folder held high in the air, "It's here." The photo had arrived. We opened the precious mail together. She was beautiful. Her gorgeous brown eyes seemed to speak, "I'm ready! Come and get me!" We couldn't wait to go and get our girl. However, God had another plan. This was 2003, right at the peak of the SARS outbreak in Southeast Asia. There was a travel ban. We weren't going anywhere. We waited. And we waited some more. Every day, we looked at that photo on the mantle. We wondered if she was well, if they were taking good care of our girl, if she was getting enough to eat, if they were playing with her. This was a painful time. We missed her first birthday.

Finally, the travel ban was lifted and we booked the first flight out. This was eighteen months after the day we first applied. The extended delays only heightened our anticipation. Our "Gotcha Day" was just five days away. To make the time pass faster, we thought it would be a good idea to stop in Hawaii along the way and then visit the sites in Beijing before our final destination, Guangzhou. However, it was hard to concentrate and appreciate the beauty around us since our focus was on our beautiful Alea.

Everyone has their "deep down, goosebump, hair-raising, tear-in-the-eye" gratitude memories. I have many. But with all the effort, all the anticipation, all the delays, at the top of my list is the moment they brought Alea into the room, placed her in my wife's arms, and said, "Here's your daughter."

Gratitude is a powerful OolaAccelerator. Its foundation is in love, and love is pure. By being grateful you will attract more good into your life. More good into your life will bring you closer to Oola.

It is easy to find gratitude in the obvious good in your life. We challenge you to search for gratitude, not only in the good, but in the so-called bad moments in your life. We challenge you to think about the negative experiences in your life. Could there be a deep lesson that can improve your life? Is it possible to be grateful for the strength gained from ending a bad relationship? Or grateful for a new opportunity created after losing a job? Is there anything that can be learned by the negative experience? Can the experience somehow redirect the trajectory of your life in a favorable direction? It may take time, introspection, learning, and the help and guidance of others, but we believe it can. You may have to dig deep.

We push this point because we know that if you can tap into gratitude in both the good and the bad that life has to offer, you will speed up your trip to the OolaLife.

LOVE

"There are four questions of value in life . . .
What is sacred? Of what is the spirit made?
What is worth living for, and what is worth dying for?
The answer to each is the same. Only love."

—Johnny Depp, Don Juan De Marco

Phil says you can't hurry it, Paul says you can't buy it, Lionel thinks it's endless, Bowie thinks it's modern, Meatloaf will do anything for it, Def Leppard thinks it bites, and the B-52's want to build a shack for it.

We humans *love* to talk about love. Actually, love has been in the title of 116 number-one selling songs. And, love is the lightning bolt of all OolaAccelerators. We like to talk about, write about, and sing about love because it is so powerful. To give and receive love produces passion and passion, is the fuel of choice on the bus to Oola.

OOLASEEKER

Option Four, All of the Above

I am a lover, not a fighter. It has always been easy for me to love and to look for the reason to love. I am the guy who gets a tear in his eye when my daughter has a solo at the dance recital. I always just feel loving. But when you are down in the dumps, life is at the bottom, and you feel desperate, authentic love is always a little harder to find.

After six months of being separated—you know, the motel and Taurus days—I had an enlightening experience. It was one of the funniest sitcom moments of my life. I was sitting in my Taurus and thinking about my life. I knew I had to make a decision. You see, to this point I had refused to call a divorce attorney. I wanted to work things out in mediation and not go through that nasty legal process. But it was time to at least look at my options. So, with a recommendation from a friend who got divorced earlier that year, I called his attorney. He said she was the best, whatever that means. So sitting in my car, I made the call. The prerecorded answering service went something like this: "Thank you for calling The Law Firm of . . . For bankruptcy press one, for divorce press two, and for criminal law press three."

I waited and nothing happened, and then I realized what I was waiting for. I was waiting for option four . . . all of the above. Seriously, I remember it clearly. Please picture this: As the call was happening I was literally making a checklist. For bankruptcy, press one . . . I might need that! For divorce press two . . . well, that is the reason I called. For criminal law press three . . . I am kind of thinking about killing one of my best friends who is already trying to date my soon to be ex-wife . . . better save that one.

I started laughing and I realized two things. First, I was definitely *not in a place of love. I was actually in a place of hate. I wanted to destroy everything that I perceived was in my way.*

Second, thank God I am not an attorney and have to deal with that every day. I have committed to love always, unconditionally, and no matter

. . . Def Leppard thinks it bites, and the B-52's want to build a shack for it.

what. It is a healthier place to be. It is a happier place to be, and it is for sure a more Oola place to be.

OOLAGURU

The Man on the Platform

I enjoy travel. In fact, it is my OolaFun. I went through a phase in which I was intent on seeing the seven man-made wonders of the world. One of the wonders I was most looking forward to seeing was the Taj Mahal. I just find the story of eternal love behind the structure intriguing.

As the story goes, Shah Jahan loved his wife. He loved her deeply. His wife, Mumtaz Mahal, died an untimely death due to complications from giving birth to their fourteenth child. While Mumtaz was on her deathbed, Shah Jahan promised her that he would never remarry and that he would build the richest mausoleum over her grave. It took twenty-two years and 22,000 workers to build the beautiful monument, but Shah Jahan honored his word and built the Taj Mahal in honor of his beloved.

This love story drew me to Agra, India. All of my expectations and anticipation were rooted in this story and seeing this magnificent structure. The instant I arrived in Delhi my focus was rocked. I was devastated by the quantity and degree of poverty. I was overcome by guilt. Here I am, another affluent American flying first class to India with a personal guide, just to put a line through another item on his bucket list.

Anshul was my gracious guide. The moment I landed and cleared customs I was immediately surrounded by people looking for money. I looked around. The crowd was four to five people deep. I felt very uncomfortable. Some had smiles, some looked desperate . . . they all had their hand out. I reached into my pocket to give some money, and Anshul grabbed my wrist and said, "You cannot do this." I listened to my guide and took my hand out of my pocket . . . empty.

Once we got into the car and were alone, Anshul relayed that if I would have given money outside the airport, it would have added to the chaos around us. He said, "You do not have enough money in your pocket to fill every hand." He suggested if I wanted to help, the best way was through a local charity. I was comforted to have an option for my guilt.

Two days later, following a tour of Agra and the Taj Mahal, we arrived at the train station to catch the late train back to Delhi. Lying on the train platform floor, with his hand held up, was a man like I had never seen. He looked to be about fifty years old. From the waist up he appeared frail and weak. From the waist up he couldn't have weighed more than sixty pounds. His legs and feet were another story. His pants were ripped mid-thigh on both sides because they could not contain the volume of his legs. His ankle and toes appeared fake. The image I have in my head is his right big toe. It was the size of my wrist. This was my breaking point. I reached into my pocket to fill his hand. Again, Anshul stopped me.

Anshul relayed a story about a British doctor he was providing guide service for just a year previous. The doctor saw this same man. The doctor knew the disease, it was elephantiasis. So moved by the image of the man, he offered to fly the man to his clinic, perform the procedure to help the man, and personally house him during his recovery. The man refused. Anshul said that the man lying on the train platform floor was one of the financially wealthiest men in the village. If he had his physical deformity corrected, he would appear normal, and his ability to produce income for him and his family would be devastated.

This trip was ten years ago. To this day I still struggle with my decision not to help these people, especially the man on the platform. I love and care about people and it hurts me to see them hurting. I find that when taking action to help the ones I love, I need to look a

layer deeper. I need to think not just emotionally, but with my intel-
lect. By giving the man on the platform money, am I truly helping him
or am I just enabling him to remain in the same place? Am I loving
him well?

We enable the ones we love all the time. It's easy to do because
we love them and we don't want to see them hurt in any way. It
can be as simple as picking up after our kids or as complicated
as supporting a chemical addiction or repeatedly returning to an
unhealthy relationship.

Love is an OolaAccelerator. However, if the love is not pure and
flirts with enabling, it can be toxic and actually become an Oola-
Blocker. Seek pure love. Love that is authentic and unconditional.

It feels good to love. Whether it is romantic love, love of your
children, love of friends, or love of community. Give it, receive it. If
you have loved and gotten hurt, then you need to forgive and love
again. Pure love has benefits that are worth the risks. Make sure the
love is authentic and unconditional. Be cautious not to pursue the
wrong kinds of love or to express your love in the wrong ways. Don't
forget to add self-love to this list. Think positively about yourself,
forgive yourself, and do for yourself what you do for others. If you
include pure love in your life, you will get to the OolaLife faster and
the journey will be more rewarding.

DISCIPLINE

"What the lazy want, the disciplined get."

— @OolaGuru

Actor Will Smith, in an interview with Tavis Smiley on PBS, was asked to what he attributes his great success. He ascribed it to his work ethic and discipline. He said, "The only thing that I see that is distinctly different about me is I'm not afraid to die on a treadmill. I will run. I will not be outworked, period! You might have more talent than me, you might be smarter than me, you might be sexier than me, you might be all of those things. You got it on me in nine categories. But if we get on the treadmill together, there's two things: You're getting off first, or I'm going to die! It's really that simple."

Rarely will you find someone who has succeeded in attaining the life of their dreams without a strong work ethic and discipline. Oola is not for the undisciplined.

OOLASEEKER

Prewired for Discipline

I believe that if people dig deep enough, each one of us has an amazing amount of discipline. Of course, some of us have slightly more than others and some of us have slightly less, but we all have enough. We all have enough to live out our purpose in life. I would never send my children on a trip without making sure they had enough gas, the oil checked, enough money for food, and the directions to get where they are headed. And, I know that God would not have given us a purpose and not given us enough fuel to get there. The fuel we need is discipline, and we all have enough in us.

We are born and we begin our mission to fulfill our purpose in life. At birth, all the supplies to succeed along our journey are neatly packed inside us. All the OolaAccelerators are pre-programmed in us. We have a suitcase full of love, a cooler of passion, a wallet of gratitude to spend along the way, and all the discipline necessary to do the right things with it. But, what happens along the way? Somewhere along the line we start to believe that we are not worthy and lose our passion. We get hurt and it hardens our hearts toward love. Someone tells us we are not smart enough, good looking enough, tall enough, skinny enough, or just not in the right place at the right time. That is all crap. If you feel this way, it is time to dig deep and find the discipline you need to follow your plan and your path to your OolaLife!

Just like you, I am genetically wired with serious discipline. My great-grandparents had the discipline to cross the Atlantic Ocean from Germany and Russia to the United States in search of a better life. They then trekked by train from Ellis Island, New York, to Kansas and to the Dakota Territory by horse and buggy, all for 160 acres of rough land and harsh conditions. It was like the "Ships, Trains, and Buggies" version of Planes, Trains, and Automobiles—without the fun. I really don't think they lacked discipline.

One of my favorite stories is set in 1946. My mom was two years old, her only brother was three and my grandma had her third child on the way. My grandfather was shipped off to an infirmary to be quarantined for tuberculosis. After six months of being isolated so that he wouldn't spread the disease, they found out he didn't have TB and he was released. The funny thing is that, even though he roomed with people sick from tuberculosis for six months, he never had it and he never got it.

So it was back to the farm to his young family, including their new baby daughter. When he arrived home, times were tough. They were recovering from the Great Depression, which transitioned right into World War II. Then my grandfather had been taken away for six months. Times got so bad financially that their diets suffered greatly. They were developing scurvy, a form of Vitamin C deficiency. The solution: Sell what they could to buy expensive oranges. Grandma and the children ate the oranges and grandpa ate the peelings because he had no other options. Discipline? Do I really even need to go there? I think not.

My parents grew up with little and worked very hard for everything they had. They woke up early, like 4 a.m. type stuff, and worked late into the evening. My mom was by my dad's side every step of the way. Their purpose was to support a family and they both tapped into the discipline necessary to provide for my four sisters and me—always! I am grateful for the opportunities their work ethic and discipline have provided me and the examples they set.

The difference nowadays is that we find contentment. We have found the "it's good enough" life. Mediocrity is not good enough; it's a sin. If any one of us faced the adversity and seriously tough times of our parents and grandparents, we would dig to find this discipline that is needed to overcome.

We are prewired to be disciplined. It is already in us and we refuel ourselves with this discipline and take our lives to the next level. I refuse to get off the treadmill. I refuse to not live out my purpose. Some OolaBlockers may be tossed my way and I may have some weakened OolaAccelerators at times, but I will never lack the discipline to push forward on my path. You have every ounce of discipline you need; find it and go get your OolaLife!

OOLAGURU

Running in the Rain

I just finished a morning run . . . in the rain. I really don't enjoy running. I enjoy eating, and running supports my love of food. I would much prefer to sit with my wife, have a cup of coffee, and chat in that sweet spot in the early morning before the kids wake. But I have learned that if I wait for that perfect time—not too hot, not too cold, not too tired, not too sore, not raining—I will run about twice a month, if at all. I have realized that if I am committed to a life in Oola, I must have discipline in things that I don't naturally enjoy.

In order to be disciplined I have embraced the concept of delayed gratification. Delayed gratification was the norm just a generation ago, but it has lost its sexiness. Now, we want it and we want it *now!* And if we want it now, there is always someone ready to get it for us, right now! If we can't afford that couch, no problem: "No money now and no interest for six months." Have a craving? Indulge! There's always a promising pill, procedure, or this cool piece of equipment to shed unwanted pounds. Feeling unloved? It's easy to find a place where you can meet someone to feel loved, if only for a night.

Improving my fitness requires me to consistently burn more than I consume. Becoming debt free required me to spend less than I make. Having healthy

> **Let's embrace delayed gratification and make it sexy again.**

relationships requires me to sort the healthy from the toxic. Growing in faith may require me to step outside my comfort zone and be open to a new way of thinking. Growing in OolaFun requires me to keep what I enjoy doing on my own time in check. All of these require discipline. Discipline is the fuel of delayed gratification and delayed gratification leads to the OolaLife. The final reward is sweet.

My extreme personal example of discipline was completing the Ironman. Again, I am not one who has a natural love of exercise, but I do have a deep desire to challenge myself and to balance and grow. The Ironman consists of a 2.4-mile swim, followed by 112 miles on the bike, and ends with a full marathon—a 26.2-mile run. That sounds like a lot, especially for a guy who just a few years earlier couldn't run to the mailbox.

Anything is possible. I realized that when I was competing in a marathon a few months earlier and I saw a woman running the full marathon with a prosthetic leg. I saw her only from behind and briefly, because she whizzed past me. She showed me what is possible. I can complete an Ironman.

Wanting to keep my life in balance, and not draw too much time away from my family, friends, and career, I would wake at 4:30 a.m. for my workouts. My only encounters with 4:30 a.m. prior to my Ironman training involved a fishing pole or my University of Wisconsin college days (for the record, separate incidences).

At 4:30 a.m. it is dark, very dark. And, in northern Minnesota, cold. A typical morning would involve pounding a Red Bull, getting into a wetsuit, and, with steam coming off the water, swimming around the lake, in the dark. This was early summer and the water temperature was in the low sixties. My exposed skin (hands, feet, and face) was numb by the time I passed my brother's dock. After the swim, the sun would still be below the horizon, but the glow would provide just enough light for me to see. I would practice a quick transition onto the bike and ride for three to four hours (fifty to seventy miles). The sun would be up by this time and encourage me on my run, which was usually six to fourteen miles. I would always try to be home by 10 a.m., and with a forced smile on my face, ready to take on the demands of work and home.

My best memory of race day was the final mile of the final leg of the race. I was on mile 25 of the run. Just 1.2 miles from the finish line. At this time I had been exercising for over 15 hours, nonstop. I was tired and, just ahead of me, I saw a hill. Hills suck at mile 1, they really suck at mile 25. Whoever planned the course must have never competed in an Ironman or was just plain evil. I saw the hill, put my head down (this is my "grind-it-out" position), and kept my legs moving. I told myself I would not walk. I kept running, but I am certain my pace at this time was slower than a walk.

It was at that moment I heard the faint sound of music behind me. It was getting closer and louder. After a few seconds, the music was loud enough to recognize. It was the Black Eyed Peas "I Gotta Feeling." The lyrics sang about how tonight was gonna be a good night. I looked up from my grind-it-out position and saw a guy just to the left of me, on his bike, with a boom-box ('80s reference) strapped to his bike rack with the music blaring. He looked me in the eyes and said "you got this" and escorted me to the top of the hill. I wish this guy knew how much I appreciated that. It was exactly what I needed, exactly when I needed it. That night did turn out to be a good night.

Anything is possible with discipline and delayed gratification. Nobody is perfectly disciplined, and perfect discipline is not required for a life in Oola. If you set a goal to exercise three times per week, and miss one, don't quit completely. Just get back on the routine. If you say you are not going to eat after 7 p.m. but break this self-promise on a night out with the girls, no problem. Hop back on track the next day. Just do better.

Discipline is inside you. Learn to tap into this incredible resource. Let's embrace delayed gratification and make it sexy again.

Rewards that are not immediate hold deeper meaning, deeper value. Discipline is the OolaAccelerator that will have immediate impact in all 7 F's of Oola since many of them require you to sacrifice now in order to win later, and that takes discipline.

In which area of your life can you use more discipline? Take attainable baby steps in this area. Prove to yourself that discipline is within you, and you will accelerate your way to Oola.

INTEGRITY

"My heroes are just everyday people who work hard,
are honest, and have integrity."

—Jordin Sparks

ntegrity is defined as "adherence to moral and ethical principles; soundness of moral character; honesty."

Who can argue that integrity is a bad thing? Everyone aspires to act in integrity. The problem is that we are human and we make mistakes. Sometimes they are big and obvious. And sometimes they are subtle and gray.

With a deep desire to balance and grow your life, and a clear image of the life of your dreams, be wary of stepping over this line, especially the gray line, to speed up the process. It happens to the best of us. We want it so badly. We use justification to act in a way that is out of integrity to get us to our goal faster. This will catch up with you and will end badly.

Acting with a base of moral and ethical principles will set you up for greatness and accelerate your journey to Oola. In the early stage of the race you may be passed by those who have no problem stepping over the line. Let them pass. You will meet them again on the way up, when they are reprimanded for their poor choices, as your efforts are noticed and rewarded.

OOLASEEKER

The Justification Pileup

I am going to make a wild assumption. The golden horseshoe that is stuck up the OolaGuru's backside is named Mr. Integrity. I am slightly embarrassed to admit that the first time I heard the word "integrity" was from the OolaGuru during my internship with him many years ago. I remember the word sounding cool and seemingly important. I remember looking the word up to grab some clarity in its meaning. The next thing I remember thinking was, Man, I suck at integrity. I don't purposely walk the earth living a life of low integrity, but I knew at that moment that I lacked it.

Let me explain; welcome to my mind. Here is a typical day inside my head. Alarm goes off at 6 a.m. so that I can get in a quick workout before I start my day. I justify that I stayed up late last night working, so I'll sneak in thirty more minutes of snoring and just work out later. After hitting the snooze three times, I wake up and shower. I take a quick look at myself in the mirror with my towel wrapped slightly below my belly bottom with some serious tensile strength. Do I look good? I ask myself. As a matter of fact I do—no need to work out at all today. Besides, I worked out yesterday. I look good today, so who really cares that my OolaPath says to work out five times a week. Plus, I now have more time to get some work done! That's justification two; let's keep going.

If you have lied to yourself repeatedly over your lifetime, YOU won't believe YOU anymore.

I get dressed and head to the fridge for breakfast. My options are healthy choices and unhealthy choices. With a still-delusional image of myself from the steamed up shower mirror, I reach for option two and welcome justification three into my day, and it's only 7 a.m. Man, I had a really good day yesterday—I am going to go grab a coffee to celebrate a job well done. Number four! The rest of the day is filled with Shoot, I forgot to call that guy; I feel like I am for-getting something today; I know I said we would meet at noon, but can we hook up at 12:30?

The justifications and lack of integrity pile up without even realiz-ing it. At the end of the day, instead of creating little wins along the way, I feel like I have failed and let down many people, including myself.

Integrity is a major OolaAccelerator and, conversely, lack of integrity is a major OolaBlocker. It is like love is the accelerator that unlocks the door, gratitude opens the door wide for all the blessings to come your way, and integrity is the rubber doorstop that keeps it open. Living a life of integrity may be the golden horseshoe that you need to accelerate your path to the OolaLife. Of all the people I know, the OolaGuru has the highest level of integrity I have ever seen. My solution to help with my integrity is planning my day the evening before and putting together a to-do list that I start knock-ing off one by one as soon as I wake up. Additionally, if I promise someone a phone call or a lunch meeting, I enter it into my phone and set reminders to keep me in check. If you live a life of integrity, keep it. If you struggle with integrity like I do, make a mental effort to improve this OolaAccelerator.

OOLAGURU

You Got This

When I set my goals as part of my OolaPlan each year (which we'll discuss in Chapter 25), I take the process very seriously. I have been doing this as long as I can remember. I usually start thinking about it at the end of November, have it in pencil by mid-December, and in ink by January 1. The reason I take the OolaPlan process so seriously is that I have learned what I write down typically happens. It turns into more of a to-do list than goal-setting.

I attribute my success in goalsetting in large part to integrity. Not in the common use of the word, which is to act in integrity with those you interact with on a day-to-day basis (which is obviously important and very Oola), but in this instance I am speaking of staying in integrity with yourself.

Think of it this way: Let's say on January 1 you set a goal to lose fifty pounds in three months. You are committed. You join a gym, buy a bunch of fruits and vegetables, and even get a cool workout outfit. The first week you work out daily, starve yourself, and lose six pounds. The second week you work out twice and your diet drifts. The third week you give up completely. Think of your self-talk at this moment. You made a deal to stick to a plan for three months and lose fifty pounds. You broke the deal with yourself by week three. You have lied to yourself and are therefore out of integrity with yourself. You feel guilt, and guilt is an OolaBlocker. You are actually in a worse place than doing nothing at all.

Let's use another example: Beginning January 1 you decide you are going to stick to a written budget. You are off to a great start, and then the tires go bad on the car and you are overbudget. Once that happens, you throw the budget out the window and are back to your old ways. Again, you broke the deal with yourself. You are out of integrity with yourself.

In other words, you don't even believe you anymore! Every time you set a goal and fail, you lose integrity with yourself. Just as if a friend were to lie to you consistently over the years, eventually you wouldn't believe them. If you have lied to yourself repeatedly over your lifetime, *you* won't believe *you* anymore. I'm going to lose weight. I'm going to save money. I'm going to stop this toxic behavior. I'm going to start this healthy behavior, all lose their meaning because the words are cheap since you have a history of not keeping your word to yourself.

Thankfully, there is a remedy to break this negative cycle. Start keeping your word . . . to yourself. You can do this by creating a "culture of winning." Baby steps, in the direction of your larger goal, that are attainable. I have always set goals this way and I attribute much of my OolaPlanning success to this simple strategy.

For example, if I want to lose weight, a goal for the first two weeks may be: No eating after 9 p.m., two glasses of water each day, and three twenty-minute walks per week. Nothing serious, but doable, and in the right direction. After two weeks of following this, and keeping a deal with yourself, you up your game. Instead of the guilt felt from breaking the deal with yourself, you benefit from the momentum of a win, if only a minor one. After a series of small wins you are on your way. You now know that you are going to do what you say. Instead of "head down, shoulders rounded" for breaking your word, you're "head up, chest out." You gain confidence and begin to feel invincible. It is all about positive momentum.

I know you got this. Now, you just need to convince *you* that you got this.

◎ ◎ ◎ ◎

Do you suffer from a lack of integrity? Do you keep your word with others? How about yourself? How about the little things?

Keeping integrity with others is important and obvious. If you do this, you will win in the end. Don't sell out in the category of integrity to fast track a goal. The guilt created by compromising what you know is right will trump any short-term gain.

In addition to aspiring to live a life in integrity with others, don't forget to keep integrity with yourself. Set goals that promote personal growth, but set them in steps that are realistically attainable so you can create a culture of winning. The momentum received from the little wins along the way, combined with a restored belief in yourself, will provide the power you need to accelerate you toward the life of your dreams.

PASSION

"If you truly pour your heart into what
you believe in, even if it makes you vulnerable,
amazing things can and will happen."

—Emma Watson

Passion is a clear OolaAccelerator. If life were a card game, passion is the trump card. If your passion is strong enough, it has the ability to trump many of the OolaBlockers, including fear, anger, and laziness. For example, if you have a strong fear of public speaking, but a stronger passion to spread a message, you will get up and give the speech. Tapping into your passion will empower you to overcome.

OOLASEEKER

The 592-mph Ride

As I write this, I am 33,000 feet above the Atlantic Ocean on my way to France with my children. There has never been a better time to write the chapter on passion than at this moment. Passion is the driving force, the fuel, behind every manmade thing or event that we enjoy in our lives. I am in this plane right now because people were passionate about flight. Others were passionate about computer technology, GPS, large-scale manufacturing, and the business of moving people all over the world. Bring all these advancements and passions together and next thing you know, a random father, his four daughters, and a son are on their way to Paris.

As the OolaGuru and I work on the different chapters of this book, I find myself writing on the topic that I feel passionate about at that moment. I have written during the darkest dark nights of the northern Minnesota lake home, underneath the shade of the palm tree in the Phoenix sun waiting for my daughter's soccer game to start, and chilling with my dog in the mountains. All of these places have created inspiration to drive my passion for Oola onto paper and into this book. With that said, there has never been a more perfect setting for writing about passion than right now.

> **Fear, guilt, anger, self-sabotage, laziness, envy, and focus are no match for passion. Passion trumps them all.**

Everything that I am most passionate about in the world is with me at this moment. I am deeply, deeply passionate about my family, my children. And, they are in a deep sleep all around me right now. Although they look extremely uncomfortable after ten hours in coach, *they are sleeping and hopefully dreaming of the adventure that awaits.*

The adventure that awaits is also one of my greatest passions. Ever since I can remember, I have mentally traveled the world. I am grateful that today I am traveling physically.

And, Oola—pursuing it, writing about it, building a business around it, and living it—has been one of my greatest passions for the last three years. Looking back at my OolaPlan and OolaPath, the three consistent topics are family, travel, and Oola.

It is surreal that only three years ago I was at the bottom and now I am feeling on top of the world and moving forward at 592 mph. Although this plane is traveling to Paris, I feel as if I am heading toward the life of my dreams at this pace. I owe the pace of my progress to passion. Passion is fuel.

OOLAGURU

Charlie the Drunken Thai Monkey

We were in Thailand with the family. On the first day on the beach, in the distance, we saw an elephant playing with kids in the water. He was obviously very well trained. He would spray the kids with water and even toss some of the kids into the deeper part of the ocean with his trunk. My kids were mesmerized. Their new official favorite animal (at least for that week) was the elephant.

We heard of a place on the southern tip of the island where you can take elephants for a ride into the jungle. We were in.

The place had a great reputation for being good with kids and taking good care of the elephants, so it was busy. We ordered a round of orange Fantas and waited at the bamboo bar for our turn. We watched the people in the distance, one by one, climb the platform, mount the elephant, and disappear around the corner up into the jungle to the summit where they are to be treated to a 360-degree view of the island.

Charlie is famous in these parts. He is a black gibbon monkey, an animal indigenous to the area, so this isn't what sets him apart. What sets him apart is his passion for beer. Yes, an arguably misdirected passion, but Charlie's passion nonetheless.

As we waited our turn, the bartender shared one story after another about Charlie's desire for beer and the lengths he would go to get it. His beer of choice was Singha, a local brew. The bartender shared that in the early stage of his business, Charlie would find the cases of beer and help himself after the bar was closed. After locks were quickly installed to solve this problem, Charlie found the empties in the stacked cases outside the bar and finished all the residuals in the bottom of each bottle. Unfortunately, this included many cigarette butts. This resulted in a trip to the vet.

As we continued to wait, as if on cue, swinging arm-by-arm, vine-by-vine, down from the jungle came Charlie. He found a comfortable perch somewhere between the bar and the platform where the tourists were boarding the elephants. My kids were in heaven. Elephants and monkeys—it doesn't get much better than that.

We watched Charlie watch us and the other tourists. He was cute, but appeared completely disinterested. Then we saw him perk up. He had his eyes on the platform. Climbing the platform was the classic tourist: big, loud, sunburned . . . beer in hand. Better yet . . . Singha! It was as if Charlie could smell the hops from 200 yards away. The tourist had just purchased the beer but was informed by the elephant handler that he could not bring his beverage on the tour. He set the beer on the platform. The instant the elephant went around the corner to head up the hill, Charlie went into action. Swinging like a superhero from his perch to the platform, he grabbed the beer and sat on the platform drinking his sweet Singha, savoring every sip. He was in no hurry, just chilling in the island sun, enjoying his passion.

By the time the tourist returned from the tour, Charlie was long gone, and so was the beer. The priceless part of the entire process was the look on the tourist's face when, after getting off the elephant and grabbing his beer, he gave the bottle the classic side-to-side shake, and cocked his head sideways with a puzzled look as if to say, "I swear I had a beer here."

Charlie had a passion for beer. This passion allowed him to overcome fear to reach his goal. It brought out his creativity, ingenuity, and determination. He would not be denied.

◎ ◎ ◎ ◎

What are you passionate about? What, when you think and dream about it, makes time suspend and instantly gives you the energy of a six-pack of Red Bull?

If you can tap into your passion, and link your passion to the life you visualize, you have discovered one of nature's greatest fuels to get where you want to go faster. Not only will passion accelerate your pace to your OolaLife, it will provide you with what is required to overcome the challenges you will likely face along the way. Fear, guilt, anger, self-sabotage, laziness, envy, and focus are no match for passion. Passion trumps them all. Discover your passion and you will not only overcome, you will win.

HUMILITY

"In skateboarding,
you're never bigger than the streets."

—Rob Dyrdek

f you desire the life of your dreams, you must embrace humility. Do not confuse humility with weakness. We are talking about a quiet confidence. Think of some of the best leaders in the world—they all possess this quiet confidence, which is based in humility. If you really desire a life in Oola, park your ego at the door.

We all know the guy with the false swagger who rolls over people on his way to the top, constantly telling everyone how awesome he is. Or the gal with the agenda that is the only way, and her answers are *the* answers, and her opinion is the only one that matters. She is not open to any outside input. Her mouth is open but her ears are shut. These people are so full of themselves and set in their ways that they are unable to learn from others. They are therefore unable to grow. With growth stunted, those willing to grow will soon pass them by. Oola will elude those without humility, and many times they crash and burn.

The kind of life we advocate, the OolaLife, encourages you to take calculated risks, grow, fail, learn from your failures, get up, and keep growing. Your failures along the way teach a healthy humility—a humility that will accelerate your path to Oola.

You can learn the importance of humility two ways: 1) by practicing it, or 2) the hard way . . . by living it. Ever heard of pride before the fall? Learn humility, or be humbled. Your choice.

OOLASEEKER

A Good Steward

Humility can be summed up in one sentence: You either have it, or you are going to experience it, period!

True humility is a powerful accelerator, but lack of humility can not only be an OolaBlocker it can also be an OolaKiller. Lack of humility can show up as a slow bleed from the top. It can also lead to choices that can crash you overnight.

I live to pursue balance and growth in my life, but there is a balance beyond that. These universal laws of balance always bring you to a center point. And, if you are not making choices in a state of humility, the universe will make these choices for you.

After all of my humbling experiences, some brought on by my choices and others brought on through universal laws, I have learned the very important lesson that everything I have is not mine anyway. The OolaGuru often speaks about being a steward of everything on earth, and this makes really good sense to me.

If I gave my son $100 spending money and he blew it that day on "stuff" and then bragged to all of his friends about his "stuff," I would be reluctant to give him money the next time around. If I gave him $100 and he was a good steward of the money, how would I feel the next time he asked? If he bought his sister lunch, saved some money for later, and made wise purchasing choices, how would I feel the next time he asked?

This is my understanding of the OolaGuru's story on being a good steward. If God sees me being a good steward of His money and all His earthly things, will He bless me with more? And better yet, if we come into this world with nothing and leave with nothing and everything in the middle belongs to God, all the stress gets lifted. There is no reason to feel guilty or fearful of money and earthly possessions, just be humble and enjoy the fruits of your labor.

OOLAGURU

Running with the Kenyans

I experience humility routinely. I used to feel bad when I would get humbled. Now I embrace it. Humility is a clear OolaAccelerator. Feeling small makes you grow big.

My brother and I arrived in Nairobi the night before the marathon. We chose Kenya for a marathon destination solely for the idea of "Running with the Kenyans." Most people carb load with a big pasta meal the night before the run, and someone recommended the restaurant Carnivore so we gave that a try. However, our meal consisted exclusively of meat, and crazy meat like ostrich, snake, and a bunch of other stuff my subconscious mind has made me forget.

With a gut full of protein, we woke early the next day and showed up at the starting line. We were very easy to pick out. We were the only two white guys in the sea of Kenyans. Language was an issue. We didn't speak a word of Kiswahili. All we knew is that we were somehow "famous." Group after group came up to us and gave us the universal symbol (a clicking finger and thumb in front of their eye) that they wanted to have their photo taken with us. They always greeted us with huge smiles and laughter. We didn't know if they were laughing at us or with us, but we didn't care. We enjoyed and embraced the experience. The Kenyans were very gracious and kind.

When the gun sounded, and the race began, we locked into our pace. The race took us through the city and then out into the countryside. Unlike other races we had participated in, the running group was diverse. My brother and I had specialized running gear that was light, moisture-wicking, and color-coordinated. Many of the local runners were kids just enjoying the activity of running, many without shoes and with running gear that consisted of jean shorts and a cotton T-shirt.

We were enjoying the run and the
unique scenery. We arrived at night, so this
was our first look at Nairobi. A run through
a new city is an amazing way to see the

> **Feeling small makes you grow big.**

sights. It forces you to slow down and experience the sights, smells,
and sounds. You can make eye contact with the people, and see
where they live and work. I distinctly remember the smell of burn-
ing plastic and seeing bright smiles. I don't know if the people of
Kenya just smile all the time, or they just smile when they see two
middle-aged American white guys grinding out a run in a sea of
seasoned Kenyan athletes.

As we were nearing mile 13 of the 26.2-mile event, we felt a wave
of positive energy. The crowd began to clap. We saw people on the
sidelines get out of their chairs and stand in support. The clapping
turned into more of a cheer. With our chests out and heads up we
picked up our pace. The cheering grew louder, and we ran faster.
Everyone began to smile and wave. We smiled and waved back,
and ran even faster!

Just then a car with its flashers on passed us. It was the lead car.
We felt the breeze as the lead runner of the race passed us in an
instant. He made us feel as if we were standing still, and we were
running as fast as we could. Then it hit us—the cheers were for him.
Then it hit us deeper; we were just lapped—in a marathon.

The Nairobi Marathon course is a two-lap course. In the 26.2-mile
race, runners complete two laps on the identical 13.1-mile course. As
we were just preparing to take a right to make our second lap, this
lead runner was taking a left into the stadium, to the finish line.

We laughed for the next mile. We embraced the humble
moment, kept our feet moving, and hit lap two.

◎ ◎ ◎ ◎

It is not always about you. Embrace this and it will protect you from pain and open you to growth. There is always someone bigger, faster, stronger, and better looking. Attach to something larger then yourself, compare your growth not to others, but only your previous self. As you desire to balance and grow your life, you will experience failures along your journey, so you will be humbled. Respond with gratitude, learn, grow, and keep pushing.

WISDOM

"A fool thinks himself to be wise,
but a wise man knows himself to be a fool."

—William Shakespeare

Wisdom is more than just knowledge. There are a lot of very smart people who are not wise. What typically separates the wise from the intelligent is experience and common sense. Wisdom is also unique because it leans heavily on logic, and little on emotion.

We often associate wisdom with increasing age. It is true that the older we are, the more experiences we have to learn from. But you do not have to be old to be wise. It is possible to be wise without having lived and learned through a lifetime of experiences. You can become wise at a young age if you are open to learning from the experiences of others.

OOLASEEKER

Riptide on the North Shore

The experiences of others provide us with vast knowledge and wisdom of the world and how it works. For example, on average human can only be without oxygen for two to three minutes before passing out. A human can only live for five to ten minutes without oxygen before imminent death. Coral reef burn hurts like hell and makes you bleed. Sharks can smell a drop of blood from up to a mile away. Sharks will attack and eat humans. It's rare, but happens more than 100 times per year worldwide. There are sharks in the ocean off the Hawaiian coast. Waves in the ocean are very powerful, especially when combined with high tide and a storm. Swimming lessons, besides the lessons from your sisters in a cow tank, are valuable when deciding to go swimming in an ocean.

With all this knowledge it should be very easy to make wise choices when snorkeling in the ocean off the north shore of Oahu in Hawaii. But, it doesn't always work that way. Especially for me!

I had been married for nine years and my wife and I were doing well financially. We decided to do a pre-ten-year anniversary trip and surprise her family with tickets to Hawaii. We had never been to Hawaii before and this was the first time for her parents, sisters, and grandmother as well. We planned to fly the family into Honolulu and then my wife and I would be with them for three days, take a two-day trip by ourselves to Maui, and then back with her family for the final three days. The first three days were great. We did all the tourist stuff: Diamond Head, the U.S.S. Arizona Memorial, and Duke's restaurant on Waikiki Beach. Then we were on to Maui where we stayed at a great resort and ate at very upscale romantic restaurants.

At our first nice restaurant, I ordered steak and was amazed at how tender it was. I didn't even need a knife, it just flaked off. I remember telling my wife, "I need to find out where I can buy this Ahi steak when I get back in the States; it must be well-aged angus!" Two things were so wrong with that statement. Number one, just because a food option has the word "steak" in it does not mean it is beef. Number two, Hawaii is part of the United States; I never left. This is purely a lack of knowledge, not wisdom. Please be kind—I had an isolated upbringing. And, if you just learned about Ahi and our fiftieth star on the flag in this paragraph, I am sorry, but you are welcome.

After an amazing two days in Maui, we were excited to get back and join my wife's family. Looking back, I can't remember, but I am sure that I bragged to her family about the amazingly tender steak that I had in Maui. Back in Honolulu, and since I was now an experienced traveler, I recommended that we rent Jeeps and venture out around the island. Her parents and sisters agreed. The sand-colored rental Jeeps pulled up and we were off.

With a huge smile, I stood on the Jeep seat and proclaimed my famous words: north, south, east, or west. I was quickly told that we were about to drive in a circle and my only two options were right or left. Right it was.

After driving for several hours, we came up to this little inlet with what looked like a private beach that you would see in the movies. It was beautiful and I knew that it was the place to spend the day. It was along the north shore and because of a storm somewhere, the waves were crazy big that day. We pulled over, unpacked the coolers and blankets, and headed down to the beach. Even from the shore, we could feel the power of the ocean. We were mesmerized by the beauty of the intense waves as the sun penetrated our skin in just the right ways.

It was a perfect beach and shaping up to be a perfect day—that is, until I decided it was time to do something active. After just thirty minutes I was sick of lying around, so I convinced my father-in-law to join me in another adventure. We rented some snorkel gear at the local shop and headed out to see what we could find.

The snorkel guy was cool, he said that he flew to Hawaii twenty years ago for a ten-day vacation and never left. He fell in love with the island and the people and made Hawaii his permanent home. After some good stories, he got us the snorkel gear and then proceeded to warn us about the danger of going in the water on a day like today. "The waves are huge and whatever you do, do not go to the right side of the beach. The ocean water that crashes over the coral all drains to the right and it will suck you out to sea like a vacuum."

At birth, there are people who just believe that touching a red hot stove top will burn you and that sticking your tongue to a flagpole in the winter will hurt. And then there are those that have to burn their fingers and literally leave random samples of tongue DNA on frozen metal to learn the lessons. And then there is me. I don't know why, but I have to gain all personal wisdom through personal experiences and usually multiple times. So, it was very normal for me to question this very wise advice. "There is no way that a current could suck me out to sea. Is there?" I was in the ocean once before in Galveston, Texas, with a couple of buddies and it was no big deal. And besides, I took swimming lessons from my sisters at the farm. I passed Guppy and Minnow and if my oldest sister wouldn't have graduated, I would have been at the Pike level for sure.

> **You can become wise two ways: from your own experiences, or the experiences of others. We recommend both.**

I figured there was only one way to find out whether the snorkel guy knew what he was talking about. So after thirty minutes of snorkeling, my father-in-law stayed back, but I decided to venture out to see if the mighty Pacific could live up to the threats from the snorkeling guy.

My grip on the coral wall held for about thirty seconds before the current ripped me off of it and pulled me about a half mile out to sea. When this crazy ride finally slowed down, I was exhausted, cut up and bleeding from the coral, and bobbing around in huge waves in the middle of the ocean. I looked down to see if I could touch bottom and it was nothing but blue. The water was clear and there was no ocean floor in sight. I evaluated my situation and knew I was in trouble. When I would get to the crest of the wave, I would wave for help. My father-in-law, who was the size of an ant at this time, would wave back. I would ride the wave down into the trough of the wave and feel like I was surrounded by a wall of water. Back up to flail my arms for help and back down to scream in disbelief. I really thought this was the end.

After about an hour of doggy paddling and bleeding in the shark-infested waters, I started making my way toward a cliff wall that seemed to be getting closer and closer. Finally, after riding one more good wave, I would be able to reach the rocks. That wave came and slammed me into the cliff wall. I grabbed on and the next wave pulled me back off. Not to worry, the following wave slammed me right back into the wall again. Grab on and be pulled off. Grab on and be pulled off. Over and over. It was almost like the ocean was saying, "Do you believe the snorkel guy now? How about now?" Finally I found a large hold in the wall and held on for dear life, literally!

After making my way up the cliff wall I painfully walked back to where the entire family was set up on the beach. To my surprise, they were chilling with Coronas and enjoying a beautiful sunny Hawaiian day. To their surprise, I was bloody, exhausted, and not enjoying any part of my day—except that I was alive.

I have learned many lessons the hard way. I wouldn't recommend it, but that's just me. As I get older and become wiser, I have started to learn, not only from my past mistakes, but also from those before me and around me. If you are a "try before you buy" guy or gal, embrace your uniqueness and love who you are. But I promise that I have already learned enough for all of us. As I continue to occasionally swim with the sharks with bloody knees and hands, feel free to keep learning from my mistakes and the wiser people in your life. It may also save you some pain.

OOLAGURU

Running with the Yaks

I lean heavily on mentors. I have always sought out those older and wiser than me to learn from their experiences. I would seek out people that had the characteristics I wanted to have in the next chapter of my life, and learn from them. I didn't hide my motives; I just was who I was—a wide-eyed young guy who wanted to learn.

For example, as I got to know my first accountant, I looked to him as a financial expert, and asked him very specifically, "As a young guy coming up, what two lessons can you teach me?" He smiled and quickly replied, "Save 15 percent of every dollar you ever make and stay married to the same gal." He had been married twice and hadn't saved for retirement and it was only ten years away for him at the time. The day I heard that advice, I implemented it. To this day, I have saved more than 15 percent of every dollar I have ever made and constantly work to keep my marriage healthy. Good advice. I became wiser without having to get divorced or be unprepared for retirement to learn the lesson.

I use the wisdom of others all the time. This comes in very handy in my love of international travel. Locals have knowledge and experience in their homeland that goes back generations. The travel books, no matter how thick, cannot possess this depth of wisdom. My simple philosophy is to "look to the locals." For example, if I want an awesome place to eat, I don't look to the advertisements; I look in the windows of the restaurants and find the ones packed with locals.

My best example of this was in Nepal. I was trekking with my brother. Our goal was to get as close to base camp at Mount Everest as we could in the short time allowed for the trip. I don't acclimate to elevation well, so it was going to be a challenge since our days were limited.

We had a Sherpa guide and a small crew to help us rookies up the mountain. The land was beautiful—some of the most breathtaking scenery I have had the pleasure of experiencing. But the cultural experiences almost trumped the beauty.

Since we were short on time, we flew to the highest elevation we could from Kathmandu to Lukla. That knocked off the first 9,400 feet. But I don't know what would have been easier, hiking the 9,400 feet or tackling the landing strip. Google the image sometime. It feels like it is on a 45-degree angle, although it is much less than that. All I know is that it is steep, short, and on the side of the mountain, none of which are good qualities in a landing strip.

I had heard rumors of this landing strip, so I was a bit mentally prepared, but as we approached I could see it in the distance. The pilot even got on the intercom to announce that we would approach at a sharp angle (like flying directly into the side of the mountain) and that he would pull up just prior to wheels down for a smooth landing. I utilized my "look to the locals" philosophy and identified a couple of locals and they were relaxing and reading. Cool. No sweat. We landed perfectly.

This trip was in 2004, during the peak of the Maoist Rebellion. When we landed, the first thing I noticed was that the traffic control tower was empty and riddled with bullet holes. We knew of the Maoist uprisings, but it had not deterred our trip. We only had one day in Kathmandu, the site of the most recent bombings. We figured we would be safe up the mountain. The fresh bullet holes in the tower made me question our decision to rush the trip.

We were greeted by our Sherpa guide, Ringi. At just twenty-four years old, he had already summitted Everest two times. Ringi was local and an expert on Everest. Ringi was much younger than me, but much more wise. I lean on those wiser than me, even if they are only twenty-four.

On day two of the trek his wisdom proved valuable. In the distance, we saw two young boys, maybe twelve, walking our direction in white T-shirts. As they came closer, I noticed they both had semiautomatic machine guns over their shoulders. All I knew was that there was a war in the region, I had seen the bullet holes in the airport traffic control tower, and now these little kids with big guns were walking toward us. We didn't know what to do. I looked to Ringi. He was completely calm and said, "No big deal, just don't make eye contact." We did just that. He wasn't concerned; we weren't concerned.

On day three, we were approaching Namche Bazaar. This is a village at 11,300 feet and the closest thing to civilization anywhere along our trek. We heard you could even rent a bed for the night. The night before, because of the cold, elevation, and excitement, we hardly slept. It was a long night. I remember my brother saying that if he ever gets diagnosed with some obscure medical condition and given a month to live, send him to a tent in the Himalayas because every night feels like a year.

As we approached the village, we saw hand-painted signs promising beds and hot showers. We were buyers. We asked Ringi if that was okay, and he didn't care—one less night to have to watch us struggle to set up our campsite. We found our room and it was basic. Two beds, that's it. They told us there was a curfew in the village at sunset due to the uprising. We could not leave our room after dark. Something about the elevation makes you have to pee all the time, so we asked where the bathroom was if we had to go during the night. She pointed out the window. She didn't point to show us a bathroom outside, she meant if we had to pee during the night, pee out the window because we could not leave. She was local, much wiser than us, and we obliged.

The room was disappointing, but it was a bed. Now for the hot shower. After three days of hiking we could smell ourselves. I couldn't wait. It was still daylight, so I followed the signs. I paid my two dollars and was directed to a room. The woman there told me to undress and go into the shower room. I disrobed and walked buck naked into what felt more like a courtyard than a shower. It was big, like 15 feet-by-15 feet, with no shower to be found. I looked around at the hand-laid stone walls and no faucet, no hose, no water. Then, in very broken English from above I heard "You weddy?" I looked up, and there, on the roof, leaning over with a big bucket of water in her hand, was the same lady who greeted me. I took the typical "caught naked by someone I don't know" posture of legs crossed, hands covering my stuff, and looked up sheepishly and nodded.

The next morning we woke, rested from the gift of a bed. We were walking out of the village, continuing on our trek toward base camp. The village streets are narrow, with stone walls on either side. Obviously, there are no cars on the side of the mountain. The typical way goods and merchandise is transported is by yaks. If you are unfamiliar with yaks, all I can tell you is that they are big and they have big horns. In the previous few days, we had routinely passed yaks carrying supplies up the mountains. Our only advice from our Sherpa guide Ringi was to take the inside of the mountain when passing the yaks. They move slowly and controlled, but I guess from time to time they get squirrely and use their sharp horns to nudge a tourist down the side of the mountain. We weren't sure if this were fact or fiction, but we took the inside of the mountain every time we came across a yak, just in case.

When we were almost out of town, through the final section of trail surrounded by stone walls, we saw a flurry of activity in front of us. There was a market in a square, and the merchants were shooing some squirrely yaks out of their area. There must have been six or eight yaks, now at full run, heading down a narrow stone path with stone walls on either side. They were running directly at us. One look into the eyes of our fearless leader Ringi and I knew this was serious. He looked very afraid and immediately ducked into a doorway. I did exactly the same. My brother was ahead of us, without a doorway to be found. And in a single superhuman act that would have made Spider-Man proud, he leapt up, and clung to the stone wall as if he had suction cups on his hands and feet, and narrowly escaped the horns of the running yaks.

You can become wise two ways: from your own experiences, or the experiences of others. We recommend both. Learn from your experiences, both good and bad. Also, always be open to learn from the wisdom of others. Seek out mentors in areas you want to grow. Look to your F's of Oola. Where do you want to grow? Don't be afraid to seek out a mentor in this category and tap into her wisdom. Their wisdom may save you from a running yak or a crazy riptide someday.

THE THREE STEPS TO THE **OOLA**LIFE

*"Working on you isn't selfish, it's selfless. A better you
is more capable of tending to the needs of others."*

—@OolaGuru

Hopefully, at this point, you have a better understanding of Oola, and feel that a life that is balanced and growing in the 7 F's of Oola is worthy of your time and effort. Additionally, you have now been made aware of some of the major roadblocks that can keep you from the life you desire and deserve, and you have been shown some of the traits that can accelerate you to a life in Oola.

213

Now it's time to get serious. If you want a better life, this section will show you how. Here we outline the three simple steps to the OolaLife. We will ask you first to get honest with yourself and get a snapshot of where your life is today via the OolaWheel. Then, we will encourage you to set goals in the seven key areas of your life with the OolaPlan. And finally, you will lay out a path of action steps and an accountability system, the OolaPath, to get you to the OolaLife.

The first four sections were intended to educate, entertain, and inspire. This section requires action. Simple action, but action nonetheless. Now is the time to take steps, reach milestones, and achieve your dreams.

OOLAWHEEL

How Do You Roll?

"Creating the life you want to live begins with
being honest about the life you are living."

—@OolaSeeker

n order to grow, you must be real. You need the objectivity to see things how they truly are at this moment. By establishing this mark as the starting point, and by having a willingness to take determined action, you can start your journey toward a better life . . . the OolaLife.

Imagine your life as a bicycle wheel, with the various parts representing key components within your life. Although the parts are all independent of each other, they are also interdependent on each other. A balanced wheel rolls smoothly and freely with minimal stress and tension on the entire wheel. It can seemingly roll endlessly with only gradual and natural wear and tear. If parts are missing, broken, or worn, the wheel can continue to roll, although with more stress on the wheel, increased chance of a crash, and certainly less life on the tire.

THE **HUB**

The hub of the wheel is the key. It is the base, the foundation, the core from which everything else emanates. Without a solid and secure hub, even with perfectly balanced spokes, the wheel will ultimately fail. What is your hub? This is your question to ponder. What is the foundation on which your life is built? What is your anchor?

THE **SPOKES**

The spokes represent the seven key areas in life. Spend some time in deep introspection to reflect on your life and where you are today in each of the 7 F's of Oola (fitness, finance, family, field, faith, friends, and fun). Keep it real. Grade each of the seven spokes. Zero is completely absent, 10 means it couldn't be any better. For example, Warren Buffett should grade his OolaFinance spoke a 10, while a twenty-eight-year-old college sophomore living in his parents' basement selling plasma once a month should rate the same category a 3 (and that may be optimistic). There is an exercise at the end of this chapter that will guide you through this process.

THE **VALVE**

In preparing your OolaWheel, your valve is what motivates you, what naturally inspires you. When a tire is low or flat, you use the valve to inject air. The valve is where you inject your highest value system. What pumps you up? Which F of Oola naturally motivates you? Is it family, finance, fitness? By tapping into what you are naturally good at and drawn toward, you can inject this power to help you improve the areas in which you are weak. Don't overcomplicate this.

OOLASEEKER

The Valve

A few years back I was asked to go on a mountain biking day trip with a couple of friends. I quickly agreed and woke up early that morning excited for the adventure. I arrived at my buddy's place around 7 a.m. and pulled my old mountain bike out of the trunk of the Taurus. I put on the front wheel, checked the chain, pumped up the tires, and adjusted the seat.

On the drive up the mountain, I learned that both of my friends had ridden professionally out East where they grew up. I told them that I was a serious rookie. They were kind enough to give me some pointers and said they would take it easy on the mountain. I was determined to keep up no matter what the cost.

Halfway through the ride I noticed that it was getting harder and harder to pedal. Looking down at my front tire, I realized that it was half full of air. Every fifteen minutes the pushing and pulling became more difficult and I was getting more exhausted. For the majority of the downhill, I was riding on a completely flat tire. I learned much about biking and about life that day on the mountain.

If you are an OolaSeeker like me, you will most likely have a difficult but rewarding journey ahead of you. The more out of balance and off track you are in life, the more challenging the path in front of you will be. With challenges ahead, you want to make sure your wheel is pumped up.

When I was scratching my way off the bottom, knowing my valve and using it to pump up the other flat F's of Oola proved to be very valuable. The valve is important because it represents your strongest values and beliefs. These are the things that come naturally with little outside motivation required. You wake up and go get these things without prodding. If your highest value system is Family, you do not have to be nagged to prepare meals, buy clothes for the kids, and make sure they are well cared for. It's in your DNA. If your highest value system is Finance, you do not have to be bothered to generate income or stay on a budget. These occur with little effort.

But what if your OolaWheel reveals that your OolaFitness is low and you can't find the motivation to make good food choices or strap on walking shoes? This is where the valve proves its worth. If you can relate to this, ask yourself, "Will I be a better parent if I am in shape, have more energy, and feel less stressed? Will I set a better example for my family if I work out and eat healthier? Will I burden my family if I become chronically ill or die from poor OolaFitness?

Can you see how using the power of the valve can pump up the weak F's in your life? If you are having difficulty identifying your valve, just look around you. What do you surround yourself with? What do you love to do and what comes naturally to you? Want a short cut? Check your cell phone.

Let me explain.

I have 1,767 photos and videos in my iPhone. Of these photos and videos, I have 1,253 pictures of my children, 211 pictures of cool houses and land that I would love to build on some day, 139 pictures of goals that I attained in business and or business-related experiences, 67 pictures and videos of fun experiences such as skydiving, skiing, and travel. The remaining 97 were of random things such the OolaGuru's sports car, my dream car (a Lexus LFA), 11 of my back tattoo of a family tree, and two incredibly embarrassing pictures that I deleted immediately and have no idea how they got there in the first place. After quick analysis, you can see that my valve is Family, followed by creating a better life for my family through my business.

Identify your valve and utilize it. Tap into what naturally inspires you. Use the power of your valve to motivate you to pump up the areas of your life that are weak. This will lead to a balanced and growing life . . . the OolaLife.

OOLAGURU

The Evolving Hub

I challenge you to consider that if you identify your hub as set in self, occupation, or money, that it is misdirected. Not to belittle the importance of self, occupation, or money—they are all an integral part of a balanced life. They would, however, make better valves than a hub. They should serve as motivation, not as your foundation.

In full personal transparency, in my twenties I tried using "self" as my hub. In my thirties, although my wheel was rolling fine, I thought an upgrade might be in order, and I switched my hub to "occupation/money." Again, it rolled fine, but not optimally. Now in my forties, I have upgraded to use "God" as my hub. It is by far the most solid base to date. I am here to stay.

This far into the book, you realize I have been blessed with many great experiences in life. I have traveled the world and met many interesting people. I have hung out with the wealthiest 0.001 percent of the world and learned from the poorest people of the world. I have climbed mountains, competed with Ironman triathletes, and interacted with some of the world's most inspired leaders. I have eaten meals prepared on a grill on the back of a bike and dined on $100 cheeseburgers at a seven-star hotel. My goal from all of these experiences and people has always been to learn.

Being a firm believer in "show me, don't tell me," I learn most in life from what I observe in people, not what they tell me. The sum total of all of my life experiences and observations is this: Those people who are most at peace, most content, most deeply fulfilled, most in Oola, are grounded in faith. God is their hub.

An unwavering belief in God provides me with a solid founda- tion for each spoke. My strong faith also provides me with a value system and moral compass to guide my rolling wheel. Health can fail, economies can fail, people can fail, spokes can fail . . . God does not fail.

I have faith that God has a plan for me and can see things I cannot. This belief provides me with contentment and serves as a stable foundation to weather the inevitable storms of life. Are you unsettled? Are you successful in all the F's of Oola and still feeling as if something is missing? Check your hub. Maybe it's time for an upgrade.

LOOKING AT YOUR OWN
7 F'S OF OOLA

To get a picture of where your life is now, complete the series of questionnaires starting on the next page—one for each of the 7 key areas of life. They're designed to help you "score" yourself on where you are now. Are you killin' it in some areas but completely messed up in others?

You can also find an interactive OolaWheel and a printable worksheet containing the OolaWheel at *www.oolalife.com/Step1*. Let's get started.

Simply rate the following on a **scale from 1 to 10**: 1 being low/bad/least true and 10 being high/good/most true. Write your number in the blank for each of the 10 questions. Then, at the bottom of the page, add up the total for all 10 questions and divide by 10. Put a dot on the spoke for FITNESS on your OolaWheel on page 230.

OOLAFITNESS

1) I would rate my current health .... _____

2) How close am I to my ideal weight? .... _____

3) I would rate my overall mental health .... _____

4) I do at least 3 cardio/resistance sessions per week. .... _____

5) How hard do I push myself during exercise? .... _____

6) I am active outside of exercise. .... _____

7) I practice relaxation daily. .... _____

8) I love my life and have little stress. .... _____

9) My meals are nutrient rich and proper calories for my body. ...... _____

10) I eat a balanced diet and avoid processed and fast food. .... _____

TOTAL SCORE: _____ / 10 = [   ]

(Circle this number on page 230)

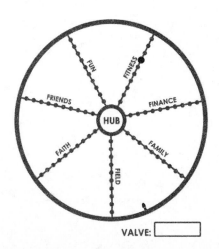

VALVE: [   ]

Simply rate the following on a **scale from 1 to 10**: 1 being low/bad/least true and 10 being high/good/most true. Write your number in the blank for each of the 10 questions. Then, at the bottom of the page, add up the total for all 10 questions and divide by 10. Put a dot on the spoke for FINANCE on your OolaWheel on page 230.

OOLAFINANCE

1) I would rate my current personal finances .... ____

2) I am saving at least 10% of every dollar I make for nonretirement purchases (car, trip, down payment, etc.). .... ____

3) I am completely debt free (minus my mortgage). .... ____

4) My monthly income exceeds my monthly expenses. .... ____

5) I am investing at least 15% for retirement. .... ____

6) I have an emergency account equaling at least 7 months of expenses. .... ____

7) I have the proper insurance (health, term life, property, etc.) .... ____

8) I give my money generously and with no expectation of anything in return. .... ____

9) I have a complete and updated will. .... ____

10) I have a solid budget and stick to it every month. .... ____

TOTAL SCORE: _____ **/ 10 =** [   ]

(Circle this number on page 230)

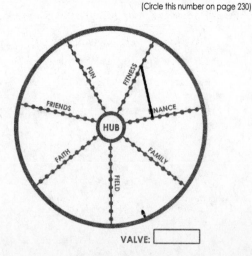

VALVE: [   ]

Simply rate the following on a **scale from 1 to 10**: 1 being low/bad/least true and 10 being high/good/most true. Write your number in the blank for each of the 10 questions. Then, at the bottom of the page, add up the total for all 10 questions and divide by 10. Put a dot on the spoke for FAMILY on your OolaWheel on page 230.

OOLAFAMILY

1) I would rate my current family situation .... ____

2) We eat at least one meal per day together as a family. .... ____

3) My immediate and extended family is functional. .... ____

4) Thinking of family makes me feel happy. .... ____

5) I am honest with my family members. .... ____

6) I work hard at being a better family member. .... ____

7) I set aside personal time with my family—without phones. .... ____

8) My family is loving, patient, supportive, and respectful. .... ____

9) I hold no hurt feelings toward any family members. .... ____

10) I feel I spend the enough time with my family to meet their needs. .... ____

TOTAL SCORE: _____ **/ 10 =** [   ]

(Circle this number on page 230)

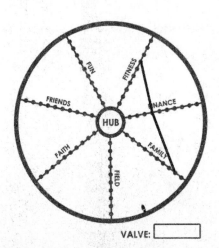

VALVE: [   ]

Simply rate the following on a **scale from 1 to 10**: 1 being low/bad/least true and 10 being high/good/most true. Write your number in the blank for each of the 10 questions. Then, at the bottom of the page, add up the total for all 10 questions and divide by 10. Put a dot on the spoke for FIELD on your OolaWheel on page 230.

OOLAFIELD

1) I would rate my current overall job satisfaction .... ____

2) My job financially meets my needs. .... ____

3) I love my job. .... ____

4) I feel as if I am doing what I was created to do. .... ____

5) I have solid goals for my field. .... ____

6) My current job doesn't interfere with my family and personal time. .... ____

7) My current job makes the world a better place. .... ____

8) My job utilizes my natural gifts and abilities. .... ____

9) My current job can support my long-term financial goals. .... ____

10) My job offers the opportunity to grow personally, professionally, and financially. .... ____

TOTAL SCORE: _____ / 10 = [＿＿＿＿]

(Circle this number on page 230)

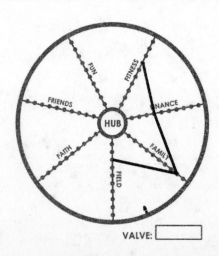

VALVE: [＿＿＿＿]

Simply rate the following on a **scale from 1 to 10**: 1 being low/bad/least true and 10 being high/good/most true. Write your number in the blank for each of the 10 questions. Then, at the bottom of the page, add up the total for all 10 questions and divide by 10. Put a dot on the spoke for FAITH on your OolaWheel on page 230.

OOLAFAITH

1) I would rate my faith.. ——

2) I feel connected to a higher purpose. .... ——

3) I am plugged into a faith community to continue to learn/grow. .... ——

4) I spend at least 20 minutes a day in meditation and/or prayer.... ——

5) My beliefs and the way I live my life are congruent. .... ——

6) I use my faith to help resolve conflict and issues in my life. .... ——

7) I reflect on my faith often throughout the day............................. ——

8) I forgive easily. .... ——

9) I rely on my faith to guide my choices and decisions. .... ——

10) I feel comfortable sharing and teaching my faith to others. .... ——

TOTAL SCORE: _____ **/ 10 =** [   ]

(Circle this number on page 230)

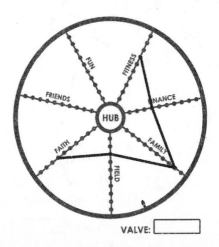

VALVE: [   ]

Simply rate the following on a **scale from 1 to 10**: 1 being low/bad/least true and 10 being high/good/most true. Write your number in the blank for each of the 10 questions. Then, at the bottom of the page, add up the total for all 10 questions and divide by 10. Put a dot on the spoke for FRIENDS on your OolaWheel on page 230.

OOLAFRIENDS

1) I would rate my social network of friends .... _____

2) I have unconditionally loving, supportive, and empowering friends. .... _____

3) I am satisfied with the number of friendships in my life............ _____

4) I am a good example/mentor for my friends. .... _____

5) My friends support my dreams and are good examples/ mentors for me. .... _____

6) When I think of my 3 closest friends, I have no stress.............. _____

7) I openly communicate and trust my friends............................. _____

8) I have friends who are good mentors in all 7 F's of Oola. .... _____

9) I have no hard feeling or ill will toward my present friendships... _____

10) I am not judgmental toward my friends. .... _____

TOTAL SCORE: _____ **/ 10 =** ☐

(Circle this number on page 230)

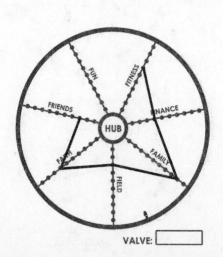

VALVE: ☐

Simply rate the following on a **scale from 1 to 10**: 1 being low/bad/least true and 10 being high/good/most true. Write your number in the blank for each of the 10 questions. Then, at the bottom of the page, add up the total for all 10 questions and divide by 10. Put a dot on the spoke for FUN on your OolaWheel on page 230.

OOLAFUN

1) I would rate my fun in life.. _____

2) I enjoy and am having fun in life.. _____

3) I try new things often. .... _____

4) I have fun and invest time pursuing my personal passion (i.e., hobby, interest). .... _____

5) I have fun outside of work at least 3 times per week. .... _____

6) I check off at least one "bucket list" item each year.................... _____

7) I am a fun person to be around. .... _____

8) Fun rarely interferes with my responsibilities.......................... _____

9) People would say that I am a fun person................................. _____

10) I easily find free fun in simple everyday life. .... _____

TOTAL SCORE: _____ **/ 10 =** [   ]

(Circle this number on page 230)

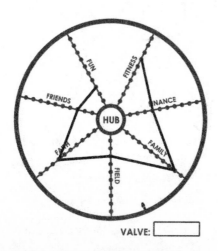

VALVE: [   ]

COMPLETE THE **OOLA**WHEEL

Now that you've completed the questionnaires, transfer your scores from pages 224–230 to the OolaWheel and connect the dots. If your connect-the-dots circle is smooth, it shows you're balanced. But if it's jagged and spiked, it will identify those one or two areas where you're off the charts and out of balance. If you've been thinking lately, *I'm feeling stressed and out of balance . . . I'm not rolling very well,* the OolaWheel exercise will show you why.

Follow these steps for completing your OolaWheel.

Step 1: Identify your Hub and write it in the Hub of the wheel.

Step 2: Identify your highest value and write this in the valve of the diagram.

Step 3: Place a dot on each spoke of the diagram. This is where you rated yourself on each questionnaire. If you scored a "1" in any area, for instance, you would mark the *first dot* closest to the hub. If you scored a "5," your dot would be about half-way out.

Step 4: Connect the dots.

Step 5: How do you roll? Where do you need to improve first?

VALVE: [　　　　　]

HOW DOES **YOUR OOLA**WHEEL LOOK?
WHAT DO YOU **NEED** TO WORK ON FIRST?

Here's where the OolaWheel is important: identifying where you're the most out of balance will cue you on where to start. If your finances are messy and they're impacting the other areas of your life, plus keeping your wheel from being in balance, you'll want to clean up those messes before moving ahead on the other six F's of Oola.

In the next chapter, you'll be creating a customized plan to bring all 7 areas into alignment. Now that you know where you are, it's time to formulate a plan for where you want to go. Let's move on to Step Two: The OolaPlan . . .

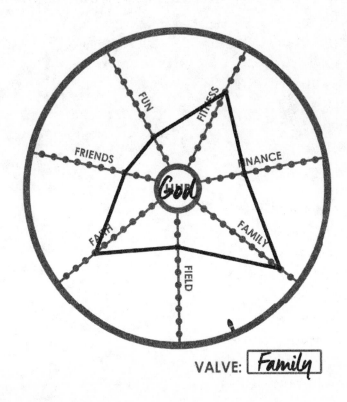

VALVE: *Family*

Step Two:
The **Oola**Plan
The 21-7-1

"Never stop. Never stop fighting.
Never stop dreaming."

— Tom Hiddleston

GOALS ARE **MILESTONES** TO YOUR **DREAMS**

Most of us have dreams. They help us visualize the perfect life complete with the kind of people, things, and accomplishments we want to have. Dreams are huge, exciting, and free of fear, self-doubt, and other limiting beliefs. *If I knew it would really happen,* we think, *what would I want in my life?* Dreams don't require you to know the "how"—they only require you to know "what" and "why."

Unfortunately, when it comes to bringing those dreams to reality, most people confuse dreams with *goals.* Goals are the milestones—the little steps you need to complete on the way to achieving your dreams. Goals are action steps, planned then accomplished. They're the baby steps you must follow—day by day—to get to your dream lifestyle.

ARE YOU **SMART** ABOUT YOUR GOALS? OR ARE YOU **LYING** TO YOURSELF?

A good way to write your goals is to follow the S.M.A.R.T. formula created in 1981 by George Doran, writing for *Management Review* magazine. "There's a S.M.A.R.T. way to write goals and objectives," the article began—and we agree. Here are the characteristics *your goals* should include:

SPECIFIC—The goal should contain actual numbers, amounts, sizes, or other well-defined terms you want to reach. It would be understandable and clear to anyone else, and is memorable to you.

MEASURABLE—When your goal includes the specifics above, you can actually measure whether you're close to achieving it or still far away. You can keep score and track your progress. But most important, only if it's measurable will you be able to determine when you've achieved your goal.

ACCOUNTABLE—When a goal is specific and measurable, you can be held accountable to it. Find someone who loves and supports you and who will keep you accountable to the goals you have set for your life. For us, this was our small group of guys in Vegas. For you, it may be friends, neighbors, co-workers, or supportive family members. Find a group that loves you well enough to be tough with you and keep you on task so you don't drift from the goals and dreams you've set for your life.

If you've ever said, *I'm gonna start a diet on Monday. I'm gonna turn off my phone on Sundays. I'm gonna pay off my biggest credit card by New Year's*—then didn't—you need an accountability crew.

REALISTIC—Where dreams are huge, intangible, and often feel unrealistic, goals need to be set in a way that they are doable with the resources, knowledge, time, and money you have available— *or those you could acquire.* This is an important distinction since most people stop pursuing their goals because they don't have the necessary resources *now.* The one thing you *do have,* however, is determination, passion, and the ability to collaborate with others who can guide you, inform you, invest in you, and otherwise help you reach your goal.

TIME-BASED—Perhaps the most important characteristic of a goal is that it includes a *date and time* by which you'll achieve the objective. *By January 1, 2019,* you might write, *I will have completely paid off my $68,000 in student loans.* Do your homework; research the process; ask experts who might know—only then can you realistically determine this time frame. Be sure to give yourself *enough* time to realistically achieve the goal, but not so much that your pursuit of the goal fills all available time. Projects tend to expand into the time allotted. Don't let them.

OOLASEEKER

Such a Dreamer

Now that you have used the OolaWheel to determine where you are, and have identified the OolaBlockers that may be getting in your way, and have identified the OolaAccelerators required to speed up the process, you get to move on to the next step. This is my favorite part of the three-step process, and the favorite of all dreamers: Preparing the OolaPlan.

"You are such a dreamer." I have heard these words my whole life. My mind never stops creating new possibilities and dreaming of new ways to do things. And, trust me, the people around me have noticed. I am always writing down new ideas and drawing flowcharts of how to make things better. The plans are usually elaborate and well-deserving of the title "dreamer status." It sounds very geek-like, but it is who I am. I honestly believe that anything is possible. If my voice can be shot into outer space and transmitted halfway around the world when I talk to the OolaGuru and his voice is shot back to me like he is hanging in the next room, anything is possible. Anything.

The astonishing thing to me is that almost all of my dreams, sketches, and ideas have become reality in some form. The journey upon which they materialized may have been skewed, but, nevertheless, they became reality. When planning your OolaLife I encourage you to dream big. Then throw that away and dream bigger.

Let me write something so overused and ridiculous that I can hardly put it

> **When planning your OolaLife I encourage you to dream big. Then throw that away and dream bigger.**

on paper, but give me a moment to explain. I want you to take time to find yourself. I am not asking you to "Eat, Pray and Love" yourself around the world. What I am asking is less expensive and less time-consuming, but similar in nature. What do you really love? What do you surround yourself with? What are your highest values?

This is not the time to think about what others want for you. The OolaPlan is your fingerprint. It is for you and only you. This is YOUR life and you need to live YOUR life and follow YOUR dreams. Yes, we need to be considerate and respectful of others, but it is very important to live God's purpose for your life. When all is said and done and you have taken your final breath, what was it all for? Leave nothing on the table. Give love and receive love and make this world a better place by seeking and living your OolaLife. Much of the process to balance and grow your life requires you to use your head. In OolaPlanning, this is a chance to use your heart. Listen to your calling and follow your dream.

OOLAGURU

Life's To-Do List

I have listed my goals for as long as I can remember. Taking the time to really think about the life you want and putting it to paper is more important than most realize. A life desired but only visualized is just a dream. Written down, it becomes a goal. I look at my OolaPlan as a to-do list. I have not hit all of my goals, far from it. But I will say that I am certain that I am much closer to my OolaLife due to this exercise than I would have been if I had only daydreamed.

My early OolaPlans were very simple and attainable. Over time, once I personally experienced the power and effectiveness of a written OolaPlan, the process evolved to be more detailed and time-consuming. For example, an OolaPlan in the early years would be as simple as one item in each F of Oola. This year, my plan has evolved into four single-spaced pages of eight-point font listing categories with subcategories. A little excessive . . . probably. I slow it down and make it more detailed by choice. I know it works and I have learned to enjoy the process. I prepare my larger OolaPlan annually and review it weekly. It starts in November by myself, gets fine-tuned at OolaPalooza in December, and usually put into final form as I ring in the New Year.

I have saved my OolaPlans over the years. I am sharing some of them here. Again, I have not hit them all. I still work to balance and grow every day.

Here is a taste:

OolaFitness (2004–2009):
Goal 1: Run to the mailbox
Goal 2: Run a mile
Goal 3: Run a marathon
OolaLife Dream: Complete an Ironman (2009)

OolaFinance (1994–2008):

Goal 1: Pay an extra $20 on my credit card

Goal 2: Save $100 per month into an emergency fund

Goal 3: Pay off my car

OolaLife Dream: Become debt free (2008)

OolaFamily (1996–present):

Goal 1: Date night with Kris

Goal 2: Dinner around the table with the family 3x/week

Goal 3: One winter and one summer family vacation

OolaLife Dream: Maintain a deep connection with my wife that endures after the kids go to college (Active)

OolaField (1995–1999):

Goal 1: Write a business plan

Goal 2: Find a location

Goal 3: Own my own business

OolaLife Dream: Go international (1999)

OolaFaith (2002–present):

Goal 1: Go back to church

Goal 2: Read the New Testament

Goal 3: Average going to church 2x/month

OolaLife Dream: Become the spiritual leader of my family (Active)

OolaFriends (2009–present):

Goal 1: Reconnect with Ern

Goal 2: Plan guys' trip to Vegas to set our OolaPlan

Goal 3: Reunite the gang for an island adventure

OolaLife Dream: Collect a portfolio of friends and mentors who have a deep desire to pursue Oola and hold each other accountable and make each other better (Active)

OolaFun (1998–2002):

Goal 1: Change business plan to allow more fun in my schedule

Goal 2: Transition my on-site work schedule to three days per week

Goal 3: Summer at the lake

OolaLife Dream: Around the world trip with the family (2002)

Remember, I'm a bit of a "no dimmer" kind of guy. Passion and focus come easy for me. Your goals are your goals. Your OolaPlan should be unique to you. Be honest with where you are, visualize the life you want, write a plan to make it happen, and stay accountable. Your OolaPlan is your shopping list for the life you desire and deserve.

21–7–1:
FINDING YOUR **OOLA**ONE

We're fans of Warren Buffet, the billionaire investor and unassuming philanthropist from Omaha, Nebraska. When making goals, he recommends writing down the top twenty things you want to do in life—then crossing out all but the top three . . . *then pursuing those.*

We agree.

If you wrote down ten things under each of the 7 F's of Oola, you'd have a whopping seventy goals to accomplish. That's a formula for overwhelm. Instead, choose your Top 7—not necessarily one per category, but the seven goals that will give your life more balance (*and* are in line with the biggest dreams you have for your life). Do this and you'll be working steadily to create balance in all seven areas. Once you've built momentum and a strong belief in yourself, then look at the other goals and take them on.

Of course, if you really want to up-level your life quickly and with the greatest impact, we challenge you to narrow your focus from seven to just one big, audacious goal that would truly change your life. It may not be the one you *want* to do, but it's the one you know deep inside you *need* to do. Is it finding a higher paying job or finishing your MBA? Is it losing weight and preventing future health challenges? How about confronting that addiction? Would becoming debt free change life as you know it? What's your *one thing* . . . your OolaOne?

GRAB A SHARPIE AND
START WRITING YOUR **GOALS**

On the Oola "stickers" printed on the following pages,[1] we invite you to start writing your top Oola goals. Practice how to properly set goals in a way that you can achieve them by writing three for each of the 7 F's of Oola (for a total of twenty-one goals). Use the SMART format mentioned earlier. Then, narrow down the twenty-one goals to your most important seven goals—the seven that will give your life more balance and which are in line with your biggest dreams. Then pick your OolaOne: the one single goal that, when accomplished, holds the power to spark the change that can transform your entire life.

Once you've done that, pull the stickable sticker from this book, write your OolaOne goal, and "make it stick" by tracking down the OolaBus on social media and personally adding your dream to the tens of thousands of others we have collected on our journey.

Now, let's get started!

---

1 Or download them for free at *www.oolalife.com/*

21 GOALS

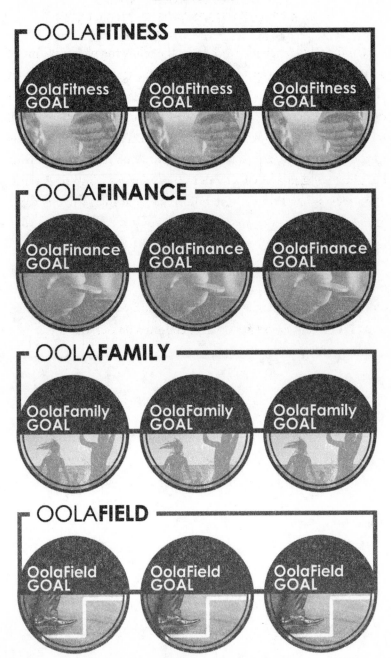

21 GOALS (continued)

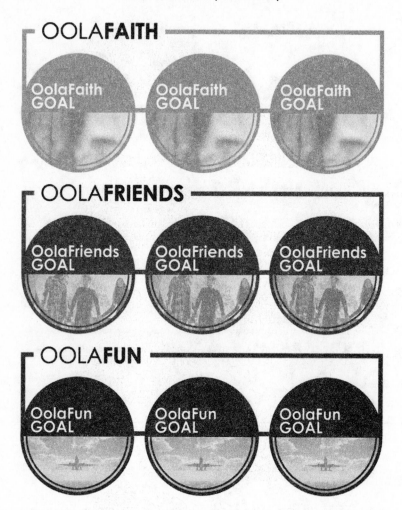

TOP 7

OOLA**ONE**

Step Three:
The **Oola**Path
How Are You Going to Get There?

"Dream big. Start small. But most of all, start."

—Simon Sinek

At this point, you have established where you are today (Step 1), and where you would like to be (Step 2) in all seven key areas of life. Now it is time to devise and implement the action steps required to get you there . . . the OolaPath. The OolaPath is the actual path to your OolaLife. It is impossible to move forward on your path without action.

OOLASEEKER

Road Trips

I've taken many road trips in my life. Some are short day trips, some weekend journeys, and other trips are seven- to ten-day drives that take me to remote places and offer endless stories and adventure. All of my road trips have created lasting memories that become part of me and in some way define who I am. After my life is over, the stories of these road trips will live on through my family and friends. Some of these stories will have them laughing until they cry and some of the stories will just leave them crying.

The main reason that I love road trips so much is that you never know what is around the next corner. It could be road construc-tion and blocked roads, it could be a snowstorm in June through a mountain pass, or a toll booth that takes Euros when I only have my debit card and some American dollars. It could be the most amaz-ing hamburger and fries that I've ever had, a huge blooming flax field that looks like a never-ending sea of blue, or my favorite: the first glimpse of the endless horizon of the ocean. There is nothing better than driving over a mountain or around a corner and seeing the ocean for the first time on a road trip. I feel like a kid peeking into the ripped corner of a Christmas present and seeing that I'll soon be getting that toy I have wanted all year. You never know what will come up and you will always have to adapt and continue on. The only certainty is that you will have a balance of good things and bad things along your journey.

One of my most memorable road trips was driving through France with my kids. If you ever get the inspiration to drive five kids from Paris to Normandy Beach through Bordeaux, over the French Alps, and into Cannes on the Mediterranean, I don't recommend it unless you buy a large amount of patience, endurance, and a current navigation system. Like every road trip in my life, the balance of good and bad was very prevalent, but the end result was magical.

Paris was great fun. The Eiffel Tower is bigger than I thought, the Louvre is endless and timeless, the Arc de Triomphe has the coolest spiral staircase, and sitting on top of the roofless red bus and saying bonjour to the Parisians was very cool to my youngest two for some strange reason. The quaint villages, Omaha Beach, and the sand along the Atlantic Coast are 100 percent worth the drive. Chilling and shopping in the French Riviera and jet skiing in the Mediterranean were obviously highlights. But when the kids and I talk about the trip, the conversation somehow always includes Nancy.

Nancy became the name of our trustworthy navigation system within five minutes of renting our vehicle from the Charles de Gaulle airport in Paris. I am not sure who came up with the name, but Nancy Navigation was now a passenger for the rest of our journey. She had the wisdom of the road and spoke English to me, so she became a friend. After leaving the Bordeaux area, Nancy was in charge and telling me how to get my precious cargo to the south of France. If you are using a navigation system on your road trips and want to see the cool stuff, always program the shortest route and not the fastest. On this particular leg of the journey, the shortest route took us right through the Alps. Three hours down the road we found ourselves climbing a single lane, half-pavement, half-dirt road with 2,000-foot sheer cliffs out the passenger window. White knuckles mixed with endless laughter and the constant "What the hell, Nancy?" filled the car for the next couple hours. We were so remote that we could just pull over, take a break, and let my daughters pee in the weeds on the top of a mountain in the French Alps.

As remote as we felt, we soon came upon a small village that had the most American thing we had seen in days. Out of nowhere the Golden Arches appeared on the top of a peak in the distance. I was relieved that I could break my oldest daughter's rule of only eating at French cafes and castles and have a good old McDonald's hamburger and fries. The minced duck, pork cheek, and veal were getting old by this time. There were no English-speaking employees at this McDonald's, but the menu was all in English and they had high speed wireless Internet. We all enjoyed our chicken wraps, burgers, and fries and the time spent on Facebook and checking emails. A challenging drive left us with an amazing experience and, again, a lasting memory.

Life is like a giant road trip, and the OolaPath is your map. Think of the OolaPath as your personal Nancy guiding you through this crazy journey called life. I can guarantee that you will have balance on your life journey. Not everything will go as you planned. You will face tough roads, you will feel lost, and you will feel that others are getting in the way of where you want to go. But, you will also have unexpected victories and pleasant surprises. The worst thing you can do is have no plan and no path for your life. Always stay inside the box that you have created over time. If you are this deep in this book, you are at the verge of change. You are at the brink of a cool new life and the ability to live out your dreams.

Over the years, I have learned to stick to my OolaPath as close as possible, but keep it flexible. When I was at the bottom, I had no plan and no path to follow. I was letting the choices of others dictate my life. I was letting my life happen to me. As I began to plan and follow a path, my Oola increased. I began looking at my OolaPath every morning when I woke up and every evening before I went to bed. The choices I made every day were choices that resonated with my OolaPlan and OolaPath and lead me toward my OolaLife.

OOLAGURU

The 3x5 Notecard

I love technology. I love my iPhone, Twitter, apps, and social media. But when it comes to my OolaPath, I still go old school. Not a laptop . . . more vintage. Not Post-it Notes, think older school. Not even a typewriter (if you even know what that is). I use simple 3x5 note cards.

I use them because they have worked and continue to work to keep me on task for my OolaPath. They do not require batteries, I can use them on a flight, on a beach, or where there is no WiFi or cell signal . . . the list is endless.

Each night when I review my OolaPath, I pull out a 3x5 white, lined notecard and write my to-do list for the next day. I put a line down the center to divide my notecard into two sections. Listed on the left are the busy tasks that require my attention. On the right are three more things directly related to the goals and dreams I have for my life. The actual action steps I am going to take during this day to move me closer to my goals, closer to my OolaLife.

Here is my notecard for tomorrow:

Left Side of my Notecard:
Drop off the kids at school
Run to the grocery store
Pay bills
Oil change

Right side of my notecard:
Four-mile run
Three fresh juices
Write blog
Book a flight for my August meeting

Very boring, seriously unglamorous, and maybe even a bit anal retentive. But if you dig a bit deeper you can see how all of those things can indirectly lead me down my OolaPath. They are small steps in the right direction. You may have to look hard, but there are tasks in there that improve my fitness, my finances, my family, my fun, and so on. The action steps begin to add up. It is like a marathon. Each stride does not feel like much, but pretty soon they are placing a medal around your neck.

It usually takes me less than two minutes to write this nightly list. Most days I modify it a bit during the day. Some days I start with seven things on my list, cross out four, and add fourteen, and end up with seventeen. Other days I have crossed them all out by noon. Percentage completion is not the point. The point is to create a healthy habit of having some purpose to each day and that the brunt of the day is spent on actions that draw you closer to the life of your dreams. The to-do lists do not even need to be ultra-productive to be effective. Some days my list is simply "dock day" or "beach day." Even then I am still on my OolaPath, serving OolaFun or OolaFamily.

A simple to-do list allows you to happen to the day more than having the day happen to you. Purposeful steps each day, even small ones, are required for the OolaLife. Notecard or a slick website, it doesn't matter to me. All I can hope for is that you take the first step on your OolaPath.

NOW IT IS YOUR TURN,
BUT WHY A 3X5 NOTECARD?

For us, using 3x5 notecards goes back to 1997 when we first met with our crew to set goals at the Hard Rock Hotel in Las Vegas. The music was loud, the lighting was bad, and we definitely didn't want to be the guys sitting there with our laptops open. We wrote on the notecards not only where we were in each of the 7 key areas of life, but also where we wanted to go—and most importantly, *those action steps we would take* to make our dreams become a reality.

To this day, we still use notecards and recommend that you do the same. There's something special about contemplating the specific actions you need to take to achieve your dreams, then writing them in your own handwriting, and feeling the sense of accomplishment by crossing off each task once it's completed. There is power in this process, and also beauty in its simplicity.

DAILY ACTION: 3X5 NOTECARD

In the busyness of this unbalanced world, it's easy for your dreams to get lost in the clutter of day-to-day life. So one way to make sure they stay top priority is, every night before you go to bed, grab a 3x5 notecard and write down at least three action steps you'll take the next day that will move you closer to one (or more) of the Top 7 goals you set on your OolaPlan.

The notecard can include the daily stuff, too—groceries, dry cleaning, picking up the kids from practice—but make sure that *at least three* items on your list are action steps that will move you closer to your OolaLife. Draw a line down the middle, if needed, to separate the junk errands from your real-life goals.

Do Step Three: The OolaPath every day and in one year, you will have taken more than 1,000 action steps toward your OolaLife—while most people we meet haven't taken *any steps* toward their dreams in years. Let's get started!

LIVE**OOLA**

– Groceries	
	– 2 mile run
– Laundry	
	– Create budget
– Pick up kids	
	– Date night
– Wash the car	

BE GRATEFUL, HAVE FAITH, AND GO GET YOUR OOLALIFE.

LIVE**OOLA**

BE GRATEFUL, HAVE FAITH, AND GO GET YOUR OOLALIFE.

DON'T TAKE **TWO STEPS** ON
A **THREE-STEP** JOURNEY

In the same way, the journey to your OolaLife is a three-step journey, so don't stop at just two. Spend time every night writing down
three or more action items that are deliberately intended to bring
about the goals you have for your life.

Simply planning and taking your first action steps toward the
OolaLife is often what will stop the insanity and make you feel more
in control. It's like a pattern interrupt. You're taking charge of your
future.

But don't just stop with planning. The purpose of this book is
to encourage and inspire you to *pursue* a better life—one with less
stress. A life that is balanced and growing: the life you dream of and
deserve. The OolaLife.

As we travel in our VW Surf Bus, meeting people at every stop,
we can assure you, from experience, that just making these decisions
will give you a sense of accomplishment and make you feel like you're
halfway there.

Now's the time to ensure you do what's necessary to go the remaining distance. Start taking action today.

The **Oola**Life
Livin' the Dream

*"You are designed by God for greatness
and a purpose. Why settle for ordinary when
extraordinary is within you?"*

—The OolaGuys

There is a clear purpose in forming your OolaWheel, creating your OolaPlan, and following your OolaPath. The purpose is to give you three simple steps to the OolaLife. The three steps will develop healthy habits that will get you the life you dream of, the life you deserve—the OolaLife.

Once you train yourself to routinely self-assess where you are in the 7 F's of Oola (OolaWheel), have a clear vision of how you want to balance and grow (OolaPlan), and how to take the actions necessary to reach these goals (OolaPath), the OolaLife is within reach.

After proving to yourself that you can balance and grow your life, the real fun begins. You can start planning your OolaLife. Think three years, five years, ten years, twenty-five-plus years. With a history of success now providing you with confidence and motivation, you no longer hopelessly dream, you can actually plan your OolaLife. How do you see your life? How do you see your fitness, your finances? What is your dream job? How about your relationships? How about your interests or hobbies? What is your calling? What is your purpose in life? Visualize your life, write it down, and take action today.

OOLASEEKER

___

Oola Is Sexy

I was married seventeen years and I put all of myself into my marriage. I loved being married. I was far from perfect and made several mistakes, but I really loved my family, my wife, and my life. During the seventeen years of my marriage, I financially provided for my family, changed diapers, cooked mysterious dinners, and tried to be as romantic as possible considering we had five children.

After we divorced, I wondered, "What does my ex-wife miss most about our marriage?" I obviously know what she didn't like about me, but what did she really miss? I thought about this often after my divorce. Was it the stuff I did for the family? Was it taking care of the kids and the fun things that I did with them? Maybe it was something physical, my smile, my hair, or my ten pounds away from a six-pack look. What was it that she found attractive and missed?

Not long ago, I got the courage to ask. I have a great relationship with her, so I decided to go for it. Her answer surprised me until

Oola is sexy. I had a chance to think about it for a while. Her answer was quick. She said that there were three things that she always found sexy and missed

about me. What she found most sexy was my passion for life and the fact that I was always trying to create new things, which I thought she hated. I usually toned down my passion and drive so as to not make her uncomfortable. The second thing was my confidence and faith that no matter what, everything happens for a reason and everything will be okay. And the last thing that she missed most about me was my notebook beside the bed.

The notebook that contained my OolaWheel, my OolaPlan, my OolaPath, and everything I wanted to be part of my OolaLife.

*I cherished these notebooks. Every dream I ever thought of, every-
thing I wanted to do was in these books. Right down to the design,
layout, and the name of the boat that I will sail around the world one
of these days, God willing. I wrote it down and would read it over
and over. I would modify, change, and adapt the OolaPath constantly to set the course for my OolaLife.*

*I have learned that what is really sexy and desired by anyone is
a person with the passion, determination, and the confidence to live
out their dreams. What you deeply desire to do, be, and have—your
OolaLife—will be respected and loved. Living the OolaLife is sexy.*

*Determine where you are today. Follow the principles of this
book and discover your OolaLife. No matter what you have done or
haven't done, no matter what has happened in your past, and no
matter where you are right now, you are deserving of your OolaLife.
Don't settle for a GoodLife or an OkayLife—go get your OolaLife!*

OOLAGURU

Pursue Oola, Meet "Happy"

I see people pursuing happiness around me all the time. They are laughing at the bar and smiling with shopping bags as they exit the store. Every commercial is trying to convince me that if I buy this or that I will be happy, or if not happy, I will be sexy, and *that* will make me happy.

As cool as happy feels, happiness to me seems transient and superficial. We are led to believe that it is possible to maintain a constant level of happiness. If you believe this to be true, that every Christmas is a Norman Rockwell moment, and every day of marriage is awesome, and that raising kids comes without challenges, and that every year will be financially better than the year previous, you are setting yourself up for a lifetime of perpetual disappointment.

That is why I do not pursue happiness. I pursue Oola. The funny thing is, I meet "happy" routinely on my pursuit of Oola. Happiness is a pleasant and frequent side effect in the pursuit of an OolaLife.

Oola is not a quick hit, energy drink shot of happy that quickly fades when the buzz wears off or the bill arrives. Oola is deeper than happiness, more fulfilling.

Ironically, in my personal journey, I never sought to be happy. It is not that I didn't want to be happy, who doesn't want to be happy? It is just that happiness wasn't my primary goal.

When I was pushing hard to pay off serious debt, happiness was not my goal. My goal was to be debt free, not be happy. When I completed my Ironman, I did not do this to be happy, I did this to be fit. When I traveled the world, I didn't do so in search of happiness, I did so to seek out cultures and experiences to learn from.

If my sole goal was to be happy I would not have my current OolaLife. I would have quit paying off debt at the first unexpected bill. I would have bailed on my marriage at the first fight. I would have resigned from my job at my first failure. I would have abandoned my love of travel at my first canceled flight. I would have quit pursuing my faith at my first question.

Don't pursue happiness, pursue Oola. Embrace and learn from all your life experiences. I promise you this: If you commit to pursuing Oola, you will meet happy many times along the way.

The three steps to the OolaLife really do work. Create your Oola-Wheel, OolaPlan, and OolaPath, and the OolaLife can be yours. This will require discipline, realistic expectations, effort, and perseverance. You will delay gratification today for Oola tomorrow. If you do this, and constantly balance and grow your life, you will not only have the life of your dreams, but have quite a journey along the way.

CONCLUSION

"The journey of a thousand miles
begins with a single step."

—Lao Tzu

T he purpose of this book is to encourage and inspire you to pursue a better life. A life that is balanced and growing. The life you dream of and deserve. The OolaLife.

By opening up and sharing our true stories, knowledge, successes, and failures, we hope to inspire you to take a first step. The OolaLife is worth the effort and pursuit.

You cannot go back and start with a new beginning, but you can start today and make a new ending. Finish strong! Find balance in your life. Grow the 7 F's of Oola. Eliminate your OolaBlockers. Place emphasis and focus on your OolaAccelerators. Be honest with where you are today and prepare your OolaWheel. Devise a plan to achieve the life of your dreams with your OolaPlan. Take action and be accountable to your plan by staying true to your OolaPath.

Don't follow our path, follow our principles. Remember, this book contains *our* stories and *our* experiences. Now it is time to write *your* story.

Our wish for you is that all of your wildest dreams come true. We look forward to the possibility of our paths crossing someday. And, with all our heart, God bless you on your noble journey. Be grateful, have faith . . . go get your OolaLife.

The Oola Wheel

WHERE ARE YOU TODAY?

FITNESS	7.33
FINANCE	6.33
FAMILY	7.67
FIELD	4.00
FAITH	9.33
FRIENDS	5.67
FUN	10.00

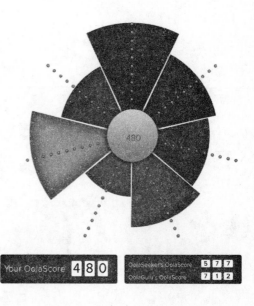

Your OolaScore **480**

OolaSeeker's OolaScore **5 7 7**
OolaGuru's OolaScore **7 1 2**

By answering three simple questions in the 7 key areas of life, you will establish a starting point. This FREE and simple test will quickly expose where your life is out of balance and stressed.

FREE LIFE BALANCE TEST:

WWW.OOLALIFE.COM/STEP1

CONTINUE YOUR JOURNEY TO YOUR
OOLALIFE WITH THE **FREE 21-DAY**

#OolaChallenge

Sign-up link:

WWW.OOLALIFE.COM/OOLA-CHALLENGE

OOLAPALOOZA

50% EDUCATIONAL | 50% ENTERTAINING | 100% LIFE-CHANGING

Life out of balance? Seeking the life and business of your dreams? The time is NOW. Join us for our favorite event of the year! We get to dream with you, set goals together, support each other, and keep each other accountable. This is what we have done together for over 17 years and now we get to do it with you. We will reveal not only how to succeed in business, but also how to achieve your full potential in all 7 key areas of life.

Learn more & sign up:

WWW.OOLALIFE.COM/OOLAPALOOZA

Want the OolaGuys to speak at your event?
EMAIL **EVENTS@OOLALIFE.COM**

RECEIVE 10% OFF YOUR

first purchase

FROM THE OOLASTORE

PROMO CODE: **OOLABOOK**

WWW.OOLALIFE.COM/STORE

TOGETHER
WE CAN CHANGE THE WORLD
WITH A WORD #Oola

READ ALL THE BOOKS IN THE OOLA SERIES:

COMING 2018

COMI

WILL THE NEXT OOLA BOOK INCLUDE YOUR STORY?

What do Oola readers find most memorable about our books? It's the heartfelt stories from ordinary people just like you who are trying to make the most out of this crazy journey called "life." Do you have a short personal story that you think imparts the lessons of living Oola? If so, share it with us for the chance to be featured in one of our up-coming books. Submit it at the site below.

WWW.OOLALIFE.COM/STORY

OOLACORPORATE
T R A I N I N G

At OolaCorporate Training we understand that retention, recruitment and sagging profits are often merely a symptom to the underlying cause ... a stagnant or toxic company culture. Rather than looking at retention, recruitment and production solely from a tactical perspective, we work to address the issue from the inside out. Our expertise is helping companies develop a strong, healthy culture which is designed to improve all business metrics, thereby unlocking your company's true potential.

TAKE THE FREE
BUSINESS EVALUATION TEST:

WWW.OOLACORPORATETRAINING.COM

OolaTea

*Dream Big
Drink Tea*

LEARN MORE:

WWW.OOLATEA.COM